The Reference Interview
as a Creative Art

THE REFERENCE INTERVIEW AS A CREATIVE ART

Second Edition

Elaine Z. Jennerich
and
Edward J. Jennerich

1997
LIBRARIES UNLIMITED, INC.
Englewood, Colorado

Libraries Unlimited, Inc.
P.O. Box 6633
Englewood, CO 80155-6633
1-800-237-6124
www.lu.com

Production Editor: Kay Mariea
Copy Editor: Brooke Graves
Proofreader: Suzanne Hawkins Burke
Design and Layout: Pamela J. Getchell

Library of Congress Cataloging-in-Publication Data

Jennerich, Elaine Zaremba, 1947-
    The reference interview as a creative art / by Elaine Z. Jennerich
and Edward J. Jennerich. -- 2nd ed.
    xi, 128 p. 17x25 cm.
    Includes bibliographical references (p. 109) and index.
    ISBN 1-56308-466-X
    1. Reference services (Libraries)   2. Interviewing.
I. Jennerich, Edward J.   II. Title.
Z711.J46   1997
025.5'2--dc21   96-54018
                                                       CIP

CONTENTS

PREFACE

Like the first edition of *The Reference Interview as a Creative Art*, this volume is intended primarily for practicing librarians in all types of libraries, as well as for library school students and educators. We have attempted to keep the book readable and practical with a firm basis in research regarding the reference interview. The reference interview continues to remain a key element in assisting library patrons with information needs.

Since 1987, when the first edition was published, there have been a number of changes reflecting the technological and sociological developments and trends that have transpired. The technology available to libraries expanded rapidly and continues to do so. Although many patrons are delighted with the technology and comfortable with it, some are still struggling valiantly with the loss of the card catalog. These changes in technology add a myriad of resources and searching techniques to an already complex encounter. In addition, the technology has changed the environment in which the reference interview is conducted.

Studies of various groups of patrons have provided more insight into their behaviors and ways to deal with them. The activities of talking with and questioning of children and young adults are being studied more closely in the literature of librarianship, in articles about questioning techniques for classroom teachers, and in the literature of psychology and children as witnesses. Unfortunately, the psychological literature is often based on children who have been victimized. At the other end of the spectrum, as the population ages, much more is being written about communicating with older adults, including new American Library Association (ALA) standards.

The Americans with Disabilities Act (ADA) spawned some excellent literature concerning both accommodating the disabled and communicating with them. Librarians now have specific techniques that can be used in interviews with deaf, blind, mobility-impaired, or speech-impaired patrons.

Immigrant populations and foreign-born students studying in the United States account for a sizable number of patrons in some public, school, and college libraries. More information is now available on distinguishing among cultures and on nonverbal behaviors of cultures to assist librarians in helping international patrons to be less fearful and in awe of the library and its resources.

A section has been added about angry and frustrated patrons. Due to security and personnel safety problems, library staff need more help in dealing with patrons who are troubled or troublesome. We talk about skills for dealing with angry patrons and provide references for dealing with other types of disturbing behavior.

A customer service concept—an integral part of total quality management (TQM)—gained immense popularity among businesses and corporations, and the amount of staff training materials has mushroomed. Videocassettes, audiocassettes, workbooks, and case studies are more readily available today. The content of many of these materials transfers easily to the reference interview.

To our delight, we discovered that many more library schools are including the reference interview in the curriculum. In this edition we have continued to include checklists, rating sheets, and exercises to assist students and librarians to work toward self-improvement and to train others.

An important and validating event was the recent (1996) approval by ALA of the Reference and User Services Association's *Guidelines for Behavioral Evaluation of Reference and Information Services Performance,* which delineates specific behaviors appropriate for the successful interview. The profession has come a long way from the days when there was disagreement about whether the interview was a useful subject of study and whether the knowledge of specific verbal and nonverbal skills was necessary. The *Guidelines for Behavioral Evaluation*, the continuing study of evaluation methods, and the growth and wide dissemination of the work of Allen Ivey, upon whose methods we based our research, have placed the importance of reference interviewing skills in the forefront of service to library patrons.

We believe that our theatrical theme is still relevant and continues to reflect our belief that reference work in general is a creative art and that the reference interview in particular is a performing art. And so, again . . . on with the show!

Acknowledgments

We would like to express our thanks to Betty Bengtson, Director of University Libraries, and Charles Chamberlin, Deputy Director of Libraries, both at the University of Washington. They provided time, resources, and encouragement for this project. We are very grateful.

Three fine research assistants, Susan Elizabeth, Sally Nordquist, and Cara Tyler, helped to gather materials, track down elusive citations, and input text. Their help was invaluable.

We dedicate this volume to our children, Ethan and Emily, who enrich our lives with their love and humor. Thanks, kids!

1

Setting the Stage

HISTORICAL BACKGROUND
AND RESEARCH

Early in the twentieth century, librarians began to write about the librarian-patron "conversation." Although not extremely sophisticated or technical, early writing in this area set the tone and basis for study of the interview for many years. The early literature reflects the interview's use in three major areas: reader's advisory services, adult education, and reference services. Each area has a body of literature discussing the interview and the characteristics needed by the librarian who conducts it.

For reader's advisors, the primary objective is to prepare reading lists that can educate, enlighten, or amuse. An essential part of the reading list preparation, the interview is used to gather specific information as well as to put the reader at ease. Among the most important early proponents of studying the interview was Jennie Flexner. Flexner was a pioneer in reader's advisory service, and her work is an example of the type of discussion concerning the interview found in the early literature. Although Flexner described the qualities a reader's advisor should possess, specific techniques to be used during the conversation were described only in general terms. It is extremely difficult to map out the step-by-step process or model of a reader's advisory interview. Flexner, like others in the reader's advisory field, concentrated on the information needed to supply a patron with reading lists, books, magazines, and other sources. For a reader's advisory interview, Flexner included the following:

1. Give the patron full attention and do not rush him/her.

2. Be intuitively alert, friendly, interested impersonally in the patron's background.

3. Notice the tone of voice and personal characteristics of the user.

4. Glean information about the patron's background, reading level, and subject interests while shielding the reader from any discomfiture or embarrassment.[1]

Certain questions might be asked about the conduct of an interview such as the one just described. How does the librarian show friendliness and full attention? How should questions be worded so the reader is not embarrassed? Little emphasis is placed on specific skills needed to help the patron feel at ease and articulate a need. Thus, reader's advisory service is a "service rooted in the library's materials."[2] It does not concentrate on interpersonal skills to conduct the interview except in the most general terms.

Reader's advisory service was one facet of a strong adult education movement in the United States that lasted through the 1930s and 1940s. One articulate proponent of adult education who also concerned himself with the librarian-patron relationship was John Chancellor. In works such as *Helping the Reader Toward Self-Education*, he states that there were no rules for interviewing but only general, flexible principles.[3] Chancellor's advice included maintaining informality as a key to patron comfort, focusing on the patron's reading unless the patron shifted the conversation to himself or herself, and being friendly. Like Flexner, Chancellor described no specific skills with which to accomplish the principles.

It was not until 1954, in a landmark paper by David Maxfield, that the interview began to be scrutinized more closely and carefully.[4] Maxfield's paper was important because it was the first attempt within library science to apply interviewing principles from another discipline (counseling) to the librarian-user dialogue. The counselor-librarian, as conceived by Maxfield, exhibited four techniques during an interview: acceptance, understanding, communication, and collaboration. Maxfield alluded to specific skills that were necessary to the interview. For example, the librarian should listen carefully while observing the verbal and nonverbal behaviors of the patron. When necessary, the librarian should clarify and amplify exactly what the patron is saying. The Maxfield concept of the counselor-librarian provided an entry into an interdisciplinary approach to librarian-patron interactions.

As the need for more sophisticated reader's advisory techniques was realized, a Reading Guidance Institute was held at the University of Wisconsin Library School in 1965. In terms of the reference interview, the most important outcome of the institute was a list of guidelines that appeared in the institute papers.[5] Actually a prescription for conducting an interview, the list began with the librarian asking broad questions, clarifying the problem, proposing a method of providing help, and taking steps toward independence for the patron. The institute papers included a sketch of the interview that combined traditional views of the interview with some of Maxfield's developmental counseling skills.

Whereas reader's guidance and advisory librarians were writing about interviewing skills, the study of the reference interview per se was developing in a different manner. Models became the standard method for describing the interview after Robert Taylor's classic study in 1965.[6] Taylor's model of question-negotiation went through four needs: visceral, conscious, formalized, and compromised. As the user passed through each stage, the librarian passed the question through corresponding filters. Taylor's model was significant because it broke down the reference process into elements that could be isolated and, most important, evaluated.

Following Taylor's work, a number of articles were written about the various facets of the interview, and the interview began to be a topic for research studies. Among the more important articles was one by Geraldine King. Emphasizing the use of open questions, King's article is one of the first attempts to isolate one specific interviewing skill and discuss it in detail.[7]

Another representative discourse on the interview appears in two editions of a basic reference textbook by William Katz. Beginning with the third edition, Katz included a chapter devoted specifically to the interview and its place in reference service.[8] With each new edition, the chapter has grown in size and depth, showing the integral part the interview plays in overall service. What makes the discussion by Katz particularly important is that the text is used by large numbers of library science students, who are consequently exposed to the interview as a topic of study. This is a distinct change from earlier reference texts and readings which, though they mentioned the interview, failed to highlight its importance or promote it as a subject for serious study.

The 1970s were particularly rich years for the study of the interview. Librarians began to look to other disciplines, as Maxfield did in the 1950s, to find models, scales, training techniques, and theories that could be applied to the library situation. Preliminary attempts were made as well to evaluate and measure what takes place during the interview.[9] Also during the 1970s, the first work was done in library schools to acquaint students with the interview as a topic of study. At the University of Pittsburgh and Mankato State College, for example, students were beginning to learn that certain communication skills were needed to conduct an interview.[10] Patrick Penland was a particularly strong advocate of the need to train librarians in communication processes. Advocating the concept of the counselor-librarian, he was dismayed at the lack of attention paid to interpersonal skills in library education.

> When it comes to the encounter situation itself, no training has been provided librarians during the last hundred years of library education. Upon graduation from the library school, the librarian is exhorted to do interviewing for counseling, guidance and reference retrieval. Apparently he is expected to learn on the job all the encounter skills

needed to become an effective reference, information and advisory librarian.[11]

Following Penland's lead, Elaine Jennerich developed a method to teach interviewing skills to library science students. With the use of videotaping and rating sheets, students were found to improve their skills in interviewing in a relatively short amount of time.[12] In 1978, Mary Jo Lynch taped and analyzed interviewers' skills in public libraries.[13] Beginning in the late 1970s, the work of Brenda Dervin, Patricia Dewdney, and Catherine Ross continued to make significant contributions to the study of verbal and nonverbal interviewing skills. The neutral questioning technique added a particularly useful skill to the librarian's repertoire.[14] Dewdney was able to replicate Lynch's study to some extent, using audiotaping, and Dewdney's study is a comprehensive description and discussion of the joys and pitfalls of such fieldwork. Ross and Dewdney collaborated on a number of efforts, including a book that extends communication skills to a myriad of library applications.[15]

If any controversy has attended the interview, it occurred in the late 1970s and early 1980s between the proponents of a counseling approach and those who felt strongly that librarians should avoid any approach other than efficient, businesslike communication. Both Robert Hauptman and Fred Oser, for example, expressed doubts about the extensive analysis of the reference interview. Hauptman asserted that "it is necessary to emphasize that too much misleading, abstract, and theoretical material on the subject [the interview] is published."[16] Oser felt that the complexity of the interview being espoused in much of the literature is unnecessary and that "the typical reference transaction is more like a normal conversation experience than a therapeutic encounter."[17] Despite the skeptics, though, the 1980s continued to produce literature about the interview. Marie Radford reviewed the literature concerning interpersonal communication in the library context.[18] The importance of the controversy was not so much over who was right or wrong, but in the fact that enough was being written about the interview to create controversy.

The study and use of models did not end with Taylor and his question-negotiation. Barbara Robinson's model of handling questions attempted to provided a framework for librarians as they handle patron questions and help patrons succeed in using the appropriate level of resources.[19] Recently, both Carolyn Radcliff and Rachael Naismith have looked at the research of physician-patient models of communication for applicability to librarianship.[20, 21] Randall Hensley studied models of learning styles and described how assessing patron learning style can facilitate better communication and learning transfer during the interview.[22]

Throughout the past 15 years, the literature on evaluating the interview has grown. A large number of studies analyzed not the interview, but the actual answer given by a librarian to a question and its accuracy. Along with those unobtrusive studies of accuracy were a number of studies that evaluated the interview from the standpoint of patron satisfaction or from the need for job evaluation. From Marjorie Murfin and Gary Gugelchuk,[23] who developed an assessment instrument for the reference transaction, to David Tyckoson,[24] who proposed a behavioral evaluation model, a number of writers have reported on various aspects of reference evaluation.

Marilyn Von Seggern presented a review of the reference assessment literature up to 1987.[25] Leslie Edmonds and Ellen Sutton contributed a chapter on the reference interview to *Reference and Information Services*, which succinctly describes key points in the literature about the interview.[26]

Important milestones can be found at the national level in terms of guidelines available to reference librarians for service to be rendered to patrons. In 1979, "A Commitment to Information Services: Developmental Guidelines" was prepared and adopted by the Standards Committee of the Reference and Adult Services Division (RASD, now called RUSA) of ALA. RASD then issued the updated and revised "Information Services for Information Consumers: Guidelines for Providers" in 1990.[27] The 1990 guidelines make specific reference to communication skills.

> 4.2 Information service staff members must *communicate* easily and effectively with the full range of the library's clientele regardless of the client's age, gender, ethnic origin, disability, sexual preference, or English-language proficiency.

> 4.3 . . . Personnel responsible for the services should be thoroughly familiar with and competent in using . . . *interpersonal communication skills.*

James Rettig, president of RUSA in 1992 (at that time called Reference and Adult Services Division [RASD]), stated that the 1990 guidelines do "not address the behaviors a librarian ought to exhibit and follow when meeting an individual's information needs."[28] He then appointed an ad hoc committee to develop behavioral guidelines. Those guidelines in draft form are now available as "Guidelines for Behavioral Evaluation of Reference and Information Services Performance."[29] Approachability, listening/inquiring, and interest are the three areas specifically related to verbal and nonverbal skills for the reference interview. The guidelines mark the first time standard behaviors have been developed and proposed as an evaluation tool. In an award-winning article in *RQ*, Carole Larson and Laura Dickson reported on the results of one reference department that developed its own behavioral standards for use in improvement and evaluation.[30] Reference staff have never had more explicit tools for evaluation available to them.

Currently, librarianship is struggling with the effects of technology on services. In the fascinating "Timetable of Information Handling Devices, Uses and Events," Johannah Sherrer illustrates the explosion. "Gopher software" was first developed in 1991, and yet this software is already rapidly being replaced by the World Wide Web and various browser software. Compare these figures:

1979	1994
300 databases	5,300 databases
221 database producers	2,232 database producers
71 online services	822 online services[31]

Is it any wonder that the literature currently emphasizes how to cope with the technology explosion and how to integrate it into service to patrons? In regard to the reference interview itself, several authors have presented ideas on including training for CD-ROM and online databases into the interaction and the amount of training patrons need.[32, 33, 34]

The study of the interview has progressed from the materials-centered reader's advisory service and the adult education movement to model development and the incorporation of interview techniques from other disciplines. Most recently, technology has created a need for yet another kind of interview in which the librarian is an intermediary between patron and machine.

Setting the stage is important, for it helps us to review preceding work regarding the interview, to put that work into perspective, and to incorporate the best of it into current study of the reference interview.

NOTES

[1]Jennie M. Flexner and Sigrid A. Edge, *A Reader's Advisory Service* (New York: American Association for Adult Education, 1934), 5–11; Jennie M. Flexner and Byron C. Hopkins, *Reader's Advisors at Work* (New York: American Association for Adult Education, 1941), 20–23.

[2]Margaret E. Monroe, *Library Adult Education: The Biography of an Idea* (New York: Scarecrow Press, 1963), 305.

[3]John Chancellor, Mirian D. Tompkins, and Hazel I. Medway, *Helping the Reader Toward Self-Education* (Chicago: American Library Association, 1938), 9.

[4]David K. Maxfield, *Counselor-Librarianship: A New Departure*, Occasional Papers no. 38 (Urbana: University of Illinois Library School, March 1954).

[5]"Suggestions for the Reader's Advisory Interview," Reading Guidance Institute Papers, 29 June–2 July (Madison: University of Wisconsin Library School, 1965), 132–33.

[6]Robert S. Taylor, "Question-Negotiation and Information Seeking in Libraries," *College and Research Libraries* 29 (May 1968): 178–94.

[7]Geraldine B. King, "Open and Closed Questions: The Reference Interview," *RQ* 12 (winter 1972): 157–58.

[8]William A. Katz, *Introduction to Reference Work*, vol. 2, *Reference Services and Reference Processes*, 3d ed. (New York: McGraw-Hill, 1978); 4th ed. (1982); 6th ed. (1992).

[9]Charles A. Bunge, "Interpersonal Dimensions of the Interview: A Historical Review of the Literature," *Drexel Library Quarterly* 20 (spring 1984): 11–12.

[10]Patrick R. Penland, *Interviewing for Counselor and Reference Librarians* (Pittsburgh, PA: University of Pittsburgh, 1970); Rita S. Rapoza, "Teaching Communication Skills," *RQ* 10 (spring 1971): 218–20.

[11]Penland, *Interviewing for Counselor and Reference Librarians*, 1.

[12]Elaine Zaremba Jennerich, "Microcounseling in Library Education" (Ph.D. diss., University of Pittsburgh, 1974).

[13]Mary Jo Lynch, "Reference Interviews in Public Libraries," *Library Quarterly* 48 (April 1978): 119–42.

[14]Brenda Dervin and Patricia Dewdney, "Neutral Questioning: A New Approach to the Reference Interview," *RQ* 25 (summer 1986): 506–13.

[15]Catherine Sheldrick Ross and Patricia Dewdney, *Communicating Professionally: A How-to-Do-It Manual for Library Applications* (New York: Neal-Schuman, 1989).

[16]Robert Hauptman, "The Myth of the Reference Interview," *Reference Librarian* 16 (winter 1986): 47–52.

[17]Fred Oser, "Referens Simplex, or the Mysteries of Reference Interviewing Revealed," *Reference Librarian* 16 (winter 1986): 53–72.

[18]Marie Radford, "Interpersonal Communication Theory in the Library Context: A Review of Current Perspectives," in *Library and Information Science Annual*, vol. 5 (Littleton, CO: Libraries Unlimited, 1989), 3–10.

[19]Barbara M. Robinson, "Reference Services: A Model of Question Handling," *RQ* 29 (fall 1989): 49.

[20]Carolyn J. Radcliff, "Interpersonal Communication with Library Patrons: Physician-Patient Research Models," *RQ* 34 (summer 1995): 497–506.

[21]Rachael Naismith, "Reference Communication: Commonalities in the Worlds of Medicine and Librarianship," *College and Research Libraries* 57 (January 1996): 44–57.

[22]Randall Hensley, "Learning Style Theory and Learning Transfer Principles During Reference Interview Instruction," *Library Trends* 39 (winter 1991): 203–9.

[23]Marjorie E. Murfin and Gary M. Gugelchuk, "Development and Testing of a Reference Transaction Assessment Instrument," *College and Research Libraries* 48 (July 1987): 314–38.

[24]David A. Tyckoson, "Wrong Questions, Wrong Answers: Behavioral vs. Factual Evaluation of Reference Service," *Reference Librarian*, no. 38 (1992): 151–73.

[25]Marilyn Von Seggern, "Evaluating the Interview," *RQ* 29 (winter 1989): 260–65.

[26]Leslie Edmonds and Ellen D. Sutton, "The Reference Interview," in *Reference and Information Services*, ed. Richard E. Bopp and Linda C. Smith (Englewood, CO: Libraries Unlimited, 1991), 42–58.

[27]Reference and Adult Services Division, American Library Association, "Information Services for Information Consumers: Guidelines for Providers," *RQ* 30 (winter 1990): 262–65.

[28]James Rettig, "Behavioral Guidelines for Reference Librarians," *RQ* 31 (fall 1992): 5–7.

[29]The guidelines have been approved by the American Library Association and become official upon publication in *RQ*.

[30]Carole A. Larson and Laura K. Dickson, "Developing Behavioral Reference Desk Performance Standards," *RQ* 33 (spring 1994): 349–57.

[31]Johannah Sherrer, "Implications of New and Emerging Technologies on Reference Services," in *The Impact of Emerging Technologies on Reference Service and Bibliographic Instruction,* ed. Gary M. Pitkin (Westport, CT: Greenwood Press, 1995).

[32]Gillian Allen, "CD-ROM Training: What Do the Patrons Want?" *RQ* 30 (fall 1990): 88–93.

[33]Cathy Seitz Whitaker, "Pile-up at the Reference Desk: Teaching Users to Use CD-ROMs," *Laserdisk Professional* 3 (March 1990): 30–34.

[34]Kristine Salomon Condic, "Reference Assistance for CD-ROM Users: A Little Goes a Long Way," *CD-ROM Professional* 5 (January 1992): 56–57.

2

THE ACTOR'S TOOLS

I was trying to look normal—to take a normal user's approach to the library. . . . So I said I was looking for some books on flying. She [the staff member] just turned around and started punching on her terminal. . . . After a few minutes, I realized she wasn't going to ask me anything more, and I knew I'd get sent to the wrong section. So I said, "Well, actually, I'm looking for jet lag." She just kept punching, but I intuited that she was getting another subject heading. And then she said there's nothing on jet lag. Then she wrote down a number and tore it off the paper and gave it to me. . . . The specific number she gave me was a book on how fly a light aircraft.[1]

This transaction took place in the context of an experiment using library school students as users to find out what users considered the most helpful and least helpful features of service. About this transaction, Patricia Dewdney and Catherine Ross state, "[It] was an epitome of almost all possible deficiencies."[2]

It is to be hoped that not many interviews are conducted in such an offhand manner, but, as with any professional technique, conducting an effective interview requires specialized skills. This chapter explores the specific interviewing skills that may be used to conduct a reference interview. The skills are relatively tangible and can be taught, learned, and practiced. However, the skillful interviewer will exhibit intangible components that make this controlled conversation successful. Before focusing on specific skills, one should take a general view of the interview and be aware of some of the intangibles.

9

INTANGIBLE COMPONENTS

The first intangible is *style*, that undefinable badge of individuality that makes each person unique. No one specific personality trait or characteristic creates style; rather, it is a combination of experiences, attitudes, appearances, and other factors. Sometimes style depends upon a perception. For example, each librarian has a perception or image to project of himself or herself. This can vary from a straightforward, businesslike approach to a relaxed, almost chummy demeanor. This self-projection must occur within the context of the situational image. In other words, the more compatible the style of the librarian with the style of the institution, the more successful he or she might be. However, a totally different style from that of the institution may be just what is needed to create a new and better patron-librarian climate.

In any event, style, as undefinable as it is, plays a role in the interview. Personal style can be changed somewhat or enhanced. Style in appearance can be changed rather easily, but interpersonal styles develop almost imperceptibly with age and experience.

Another feature of interviewing that must be considered is something called *isolation*. One of the most difficult lessons to teach a beginning reference student or librarian is to conduct the interview without thinking about what sources might answer the question. Psychologically, the librarian must concentrate totally on the interview. This concentration is difficult given the busy climate of most libraries. The librarian must use verbal and nonverbal skills to determine exactly what the patron wants. The questioning and listening must take place *before* moving on to answering the patron's question (through whatever means available). As a librarian conducts more interviews, he or she realizes why isolation of the interview at its early stages is, in the long run, more efficient and effective than trying to answer a request before it is fully understood.

The third intangible is *success*. Many successful interviews may conclude without the patron finding the necessary information. Perhaps the information does not exist in the format the patron wants, or the library cannot supply the information. Maybe the patron just wants someone to talk with. In any event, a successful interview is one in which the patron feels satisfied that the librarian has given undivided attention and provided competent services. This may be quite different from what a librarian has traditionally considered successful: that the question has been answered completely.

TANGIBLE COMPONENTS

Beyond the intangibles are some specific skills that can be identified, studied, and practiced. We believe that 12 skills must be learned to conduct a successful interview.

Nonverbal Skills

- Eye contact
- Gestures
- Posture
- Facial expression and tone of voice

Verbal Skills

- Remembering
- Avoiding premature diagnoses
- Reflecting feelings verbally
- Restating or paraphrasing content
- Using encouragers
- Closing
- Giving opinions and suggestions
- Asking open questions

Much of the credit for the early work of identifying specific interviewing skills must go to Allen Ivey's work in microcounseling at the University of Massachusetts.[3] Using Ivey's innovative approach, Elaine Jennerich modified these skills so they might be more appropriately applied to librarianship.[4] Because Ivey's original work applied to counseling, he could assume that clients made appointments, that interviews lasted a long time, and that the nature of the client's need was generally personal and private. Using library school graduate students, Elaine Jennerich developed an experiment to improve students' interviewing skills. Based on the success of that experiment, Edward Jennerich used the technique successfully with library science students.[5] The 12 skills are appropriate to librarianship and do result in more effective reference interviews.

Ivey's work has continued to gain influence and to be adapted to many disciplines in which professionals and clients interact. By 1978, more than 150 studies had used the microcounseling models. During the 1980s, the first and second editions of the microcounseling books were the second most cited books of the decade in the field of counseling.[6] Basic attending skills, as Ivey calls them, are now routinely taught in counseling, social work, and other helping professions. A particularly useful book that gives specific instructions as to ways to teach interviewing skills is *Basic Attending Skills*,[7] now in its third edition. For example, a basic microskill format is outlined using

- warm-up/orientation
- reading

- viewing of video model or live demonstration
- practice
- do-use-teach
- evaluation

Nonverbal Skills

Nonverbal skills, which are the easiest to learn and retain, are in many cases already part of the style and demeanor of people in a service profession. They can easily be practiced in everyday conversation with family and friends.

"By far the most powerful nonverbal communication is *eye contact*."[8] In American culture, it is preferable to look straight into the eyes of the person to whom one is speaking. To speak to a person who does not do so is disconcerting. In conducting the interview, however, it is wise to remember that not all cultures share this behavior; in fact, someone who is extremely shy or embarrassed may not be able to establish eye contact. Whatever the situation, the librarian should do his or her best to make and maintain eye contact with the patron throughout the interview. Such eye contact is much easier to maintain if patron and librarian are on the same level. If at a reference desk, the librarian should either rise or ask the patron to sit. For children, a librarian might keep a low stool handy to sit on, or might place a step in front of the reference desk to enable the child to come up to eye level. (The reference "desk" and the setting of reference interviews are discussed further in chapter 6.)

The second nonverbal skill is the use of *gestures*, that is, using appropriate ones and avoiding distracting ones. A shrug of the shoulders or nod of the head should match what is being said. Nothing is more confusing to a patron than the librarian nodding his or her head in assent while listening and then saying, "No, I don't understand." Everyone has some nervous habit or distracting gesture that is almost unconscious. It may be nail biting, hair twisting, pencil tapping, ear pulling, or any number of other habits. Try to curtail such habits so the patron will not be distracted. The patron, however, may display any number of distracting habits, and the librarian will have to ignore them as much as possible.

How can you identify your own distracting habits? Ask family or friends to identify them. Or, if possible, view yourself on videotape, where such habits will be obvious. Most people probably already know they have such habits and need only apply a little conscious attention to curtail them.

A third nonverbal skill is *posture*. Use a relaxed posture. A stiff, ill-at-ease appearance can hamper communication. Some body movements lend themselves to successful interaction, whereas others do not. Slight leaning toward the patron, for example, conveys interest. In contrast, leaning back with crossed arms may signal a lack of interest in what the person is saying.

A fourth nonverbal skill is the correct use of *facial expression* and *tone of voice*. Although you will not want to reflect anger or frustration, you do want to show empathy and sincerity when the patron shows strong emotions. Smiling or laughing at a humorous remark the patron makes is certainly in order, just as looking concerned when a person is worried or sad is appropriate. Tone of voice is also important. While saying, "I can see that you are confused," a librarian should look and sound concerned.

"[W]ords carry less than 35 percent of the meaning in a two-person conversation, while more than 65 percent comes from the nonverbal aspects." [9] Nonverbal messages can be received through our senses of sight (facial expression, eye contact, appearance), sound (tone of voice), or smell (perfume, body odor).

Nonverbal behavior and the study of body language were popular topics during the 1970s and still are today. Many popular psychology books are useful as general overviews of nonverbal behaviors. Such important scholarly works as Edward Hall's *The Silent Language*[10] have become classics in the field. An interesting work that is particularly relevant, as many reference interviews are between people meeting for the first time, is Chris Kleinke's *First Impressions.*[11] In a lighter vein, Julius Fast's *Body Language*[12] is the book that popularized the topic. Although a great deal of misunderstanding could result from strict adherence to rules for trying to "read" someone else's behavior, nonverbal behavior does play a part in communication and should be taken seriously but sensibly.

Verbal Skills

Verbal skills are much more difficult to isolate and to master. Each skill should be worked on separately and then gradually woven into a pattern of interviewing. No matter how skilled an interviewer becomes, the verbal skills should be reviewed and revitalized periodically.

The first skill is *remembering*. The librarian should listen to what the patron says in order to put the pieces of the puzzle together as the interview progresses. "Research shows that most people listen at 25 percent efficiency. That doesn't mean they actually heard 25 percent of what was said; that means that of what they heard, they got 25 percent of it right." [13] If the patron keeps correcting the librarian or repeating the same information, it is probably because the librarian needs to sharpen his or her memory and listening skills. A good memory is, in fact, one of the traits of a successful reference librarian. However, remembering during the reference interview is a bit different. This is when the intangible feature called isolation comes into play. If the conversation is kept in isolation—that is, the librarian is not mentally rummaging for possible sources to answer the question—remembering becomes easier. Clear remembering keeps the patron from becoming too frustrated by having to repeat information more than once.

Exactly what types of information should be gleaned and remembered? Dates or time periods, acceptable formats, names of people and places, and other pertinent information are important. A talkative patron will give so much information that there will be a great deal of sorting to do. A child might give information rather disjointedly and in no particular order. Hence, remembering during the interview can be complicated. It takes deep concentration: a sorting out of relevant information and the ability to retain that pertinent information.

A second verbal skill is *avoiding premature diagnoses*; that is, making assumptions about the patron or the query before the patron has given all the necessary information. This skill becomes easier and easier to forget as one becomes more proficient at interviewing and the longer one works with a particular clientele. On a college campus, for example, it is easy to make assumptions about a patron who is of a certain age, dressed in a certain way, and begins to ask what seems to be exactly what the previous patron asked. By judging too quickly, it is easy to be caught off guard by a totally different inquiry than expected. Likewise, judging a patron's social status, level of sophistication, or intelligence solely on appearance can lead to embarrassing and unproductive results. Obviously, during the course of the interview, the reference librarian can begin to evaluate the needs of the patron and appropriate ways to satisfy those needs. It is best, however, to treat each new patron as an entirely new territory to be explored. Make no assumptions until it is feasible and responsible to do so.

The skill of *reflecting feelings verbally* is often controversial among librarians. Many librarians believe that trying to understand the patron's feelings and reflect them requires too much counseling and not enough professional reference work. Quite honestly, successful interviews can be conducted without this skill. If a reference librarian feels strongly that he or she does not want to try to reflect the patron's feelings verbally, it is probably best not to do so at the risk of sounding insincere or awkward. However, reflecting feelings verbally is often a good method to keep the patron talking. Phrases such as "A new library can be confusing" or "I can tell you're frustrated. May I help?" can do much to relax a patron and set a tone of empathy. Statements of reflective feelings can be constructed with introductory phrases, such as "It sounds as if you feel . . . ," or "Maybe you feel . . . ," or "I sense that you are feeling a bit . . . ." The appropriate adjective can complete the thought (e.g., happy, frustrated, discouraged, confused, etc.).[14] It must be stressed that this skill should be integrated into a librarian's overall technique, as it is useful in alleviating patrons' anxiety over the problems they have and the need to ask someone for help.

Restating or paraphrasing the content of the interview is a critical verbal skill. As the librarian restates what the patron has asked, the query is clarified in both the librarian's and the patron's mind. Often during a particularly complex interview, restatement must be done several times until both parties understand exactly what is wanted. Requesting information is difficult and restatement is a primary means of easing the difficulty. Ross and Dewdney suggest that a common structure for use in paraphrasing can be to start the restatement with a clause such as

- It sounds like . . .

- So you think . . .

- You're saying . . .

- You mean . . .

- As you see it . . .
- As I understand you . . .[15]

During a short interview in which the patron has been straightforward and open, restatement may not be necessary, but it is still generally a good idea.

Using *encouragers* is a verbal skill that is surprisingly effective in its simplicity. It involves responding to a patron with short phrases to encourage the patron to continue. Short phrases, such as "Oh?" "So?" "Then?" "And?" "Tell me more" or "Give me an example" are quite useful. Encouragers keep the patron talking and the librarian listening, and in the initial stages of the interview, that is the desirable pattern.

The skill of *closing* is easy to develop but also easy to forget when there is an extremely talkative patron and a line of patrons waiting to be served. Closure does *not* mean that the interviewer interrupts in the middle of a sentence or changes the subject abruptly. It also does not mean that the librarian cuts the patron off in a rude or insensitive manner. This is generally just good manners for any conversation. The pressure of busy reference service, however, cannot be denied. Using nonverbal and verbal skills will move an interview along, but some information requests just take longer to negotiate than others. What the librarian must believe is that the patron is not *taking* time, but that the librarian is *giving* time. Psychologically, the difference between taking and giving projects a positive rather than a grudging or harried atmosphere.

Reasons and techniques for closing the reference interview are explored by Christopher Nolan. He correctly states that very little has been written about the close of the interview and how it should take place. He suggests that there are generally three reasons why interviews terminate.

First, there is knowledge-related closure, which may result from successfully answering a question; finding that the question cannot be answered through the library's resources, in which case a referral may or may not be made; or finding that the information cannot be provided in the form the patron wants.

Second, there are interpersonal communication-related closures. Reasons for such closures may be the level of interest the librarian has in serving that patron or in the subject matter; the librarian's need to confer with a colleague; an "internal clock" that makes the librarian feel the encounter should end; or just a plain "bad day" when the interview does not go smoothly and is closed out of frustration or futility.

Third, interviews may be closed for policy and institutional factors. Such factors may include time of day; number of people waiting; cost (e.g., database searching); priority given to primary clientele; or, having taught the patron how to use a tool, being able to leave the patron to work alone. Nolan goes on to offer tips about facilitating a successful closing of the interview.

1. Tell the patron what information is needed to go on with the interview.

2. Encourage the patron to return for further help.

3. If useful, confer with a reference colleague.

4. End unsuccessful interviews with a referral.

5. Be sure to ask patrons if they have everything they need.[16]

Giving opinions and suggestions to a patron is a twofold skill. On the one hand, a librarian should not make suggestions about a problem in the form, "If I were you, I would . . . ." This is in reference to the actual inquiry or problem, *not* the means of finding information. For example, a patron asks about information on nearby summer camps for a disabled child. The librarian should certainly offer suggestions and guidance in terms of tools to be used, agencies to be contacted, and so forth. On the other hand, to specifically recommend a course of action for the child is another matter.

Particularly sensitive are legal, medical, and business matters. Fortunately, ALA has specific guidelines available to assist librarians in handling patrons' requests.[17] The guidelines fall into three main categories: the role of the librarian in answering questions, information about sources, and telephone or mail reference.

The role of the librarian is not to interpret or evaluate medical, legal, or business information for the patron. Librarians may advise patrons about the merits of a particular source and should provide the patron with the most current information available. All patron requests should remain confidential, and librarians should be tactful and impartial in dealing with requests for information.

The sources used to provide information for legal, medical, or business information should be as up-to-date as possible and include sources in the library and out of the library, such as agencies, electronic services, brochures, and appropriate professionals.

Telephone and mail reference queries can be easily misinterpreted. Only factual information should be given out on the telephone, and brief information should be read aloud without interpretation. Mail questions should be answered with full citations or photocopied materials.

The final verbal skill is the most difficult to master and requires planning, preparation, and integration into the interview's technique. This skill is that of *asking open questions*. Open questions require more than "yes" or "no" answers and give the patron an unlimited choice of answers. Formulating open questions on the spot is a skill that takes practice, so it is wise to consider possible open questions independently, write them down, and then try to use them in interviews. Discard questions that seem unnatural and keep those that fit your style. Open questions and encouragers can function in the same way by encouraging the patron to keep talking about the information needed.

> Open questions save time because they give users the chance to focus immediately on whatever is important to *them*. Guessing with a series of closed questions that also may be making assumptions takes longer and can be frustrating for both the librarian and the user.

Open questions, on the other hand, are questions that users can answer because they allow users to select the conversational ground.[18]

Open questions also give the librarian the opportunity to explain why more information is needed. An encourager such as "Tell me more" keeps the patron talking, but an open phrase such as "I'd like to help you find the best possible information. Can you tell me more about your subject?" also explains to the patron why you want to know. As an interview progresses, the librarian's questions will probably become more pointed, but the first question a librarian asks in an interview should generally be an open question. Table 2-1 is a list of possible open questions gleaned from the authors' experience and the literature.[19, 20] It is certainly not definitive— every librarian can probably formulate several more—but the list should give a good idea of what is meant by open. "Open questions begin with question words like what, when, how, who, where. Closed questions begin with is, do, has, can, will."[21]

Open questions, then, keep the patron focused on the subject and talking about it, which is the perfect combination to elicit information the librarian needs.

INTERVIEWING TEST AND CHECKLIST

The test in table 2-2 on page 19 is designed to help the interviewer think seriously about specific interviewing techniques in light of the 12 basic nonverbal and verbal skills. After the test, the interviewer should have a better idea of (1) skills he

---

Table 2-1. Open Questions

1. What do you mean by _____?
2. What further clues can you give me?
3. What examples can you give me?
4. I'm not familiar with _____? Can you explain it to me?
5. What is it you want to know about _____?
6. How will you use the information? That will help me with our search.
7. Where did you hear or read about _____?
8. Who was _____?
9. Where have you checked for information so far?
10. What do you already know about _____?
11. Why does _____ interest you? or
    What about _____ interests you? or
    Why are you interested in _____?

or she never even thought about, (2) skills he or she does well, and (3) skills that need improvement. An interviewer should be able to use the information in this book to learn and refine interviewing skills. The second list (table 2-3 on page 20) serves as a quick reminder (daily, weekly, or monthly) of the skills involved in public service interviews.

A number of other authors in librarianship have presented additional skills that may be added to the librarian's repertoire, or have verified and discussed further many of the 12 skills already mentioned. For instance, librarian self-disclosure is an ability that Markham, Stirling, and Smith believe can enhance communication during the reference interview. Quoting Sidney Jourard, an expert in this area, *self-disclosure* is defined as "sharing with another person how you feel about something he has done or said, or how you feel about events that have just taken place."[22] There seems to be some enhancement of the reference interview when self-disclosure is used, but more study is needed.

Neutral questioning is an important technique first developed by Brenda Dervin in the area of communications, and its application to the reference interview is quite appropriate. "Neutral questions are a subset of open questions. Open in form, they guide the conversation along dimensions that are relevant to all information-seeking situations. The neutral questioning strategy directs the librarian to learn from the user the nature of the underlying situation, the gaps faced, and the expected uses."[23] Based on a sense-making model, neutral questions help the librarian to control the direction of the interview better and to focus the user's thoughts more specifically on exactly what is needed. Some examples of neutral questions from various sources illustrate the technique. Neutral questions are not meant to be the only questions asked in the interview but are used as the situation warrants. Examples of neutral questions, from a variety of sources, follow.[24, 25, 26]

To assess the situation or find out how the user sees the situation, ask

- Where would you like to begin?
- Where do you see yourself going with this?
- Tell me how this problem arose.
- What have you done so far about this question?

To assess the gaps, ask

- What would you like to know about _____?
- What seems to be missing in your understanding of _____?
- What are you trying to understand?

To assess the users or kind of help wanted, ask

- How would this help you?
- If you could have exactly the help you wanted, what would it be?
- What would help you?

Table 2-2. Interviewing Test

Take this test regarding the 12 basic reference interviewing skills. Some questions require longer answers than others. The purpose of the test is to make you think about your interviewing skills honestly.

1. Do I make eye contact with each patron?
2. Do I try to maintain eye contact with each patron?
3. Do I try to be at eye level with each patron? If the answer is no, why not?
4. Do I have any distracting habits (nail biting, hair twisting, etc.)? What are they?
5. Am I physically relaxed during an interview?
6. Do I try to reflect the mood of the patron in my facial expression?
7. Do I keep my tone of voice sincere?
8. Do I have to ask patrons for information they have already given me?
9. Do I hear patrons incorrectly?
10. Do I have trouble remembering important points?
11. Do I tend to make too many assumptions about a patron right away?
12. Is the clientele I serve relatively homogeneous? What are some assumptions about this clientele that are easy to make, but may be false (age, occupation, student, social status)?
13. What are some assumptions about the information needs of this clientele that may be false (reading level, term papers, class assignments)?
14. Do I believe that I should try to reflect a patron's feelings verbally? If not, why not?
15. Are there specific times that it would be advantageous to reflect a patron's feelings? Name several.
16. Do I restate what the patron wants? Am I usually accurate when I do so?
17. Do I often use encouragers? Which ones?
18. Do I interrupt patrons to hurry them along?
19. Do I ask open questions?
20. Have I thought up several general open questions that might be useful?

Table 2-3. Interviewing Reminders

_____ Maintain eye contact.
_____ Watch those bad habits!
_____ Relax.
_____ Keep your tone of voice and facial expression honest and sincere.
_____ Remember!
_____ Don't assume anything.
_____ Reflect feelings verbally.
_____ Restate the information request.
_____ Encourage the patron with "And?" "Oh?" and "Tell me more."
_____ Don't interrupt.
_____ ASK OPEN QUESTIONS!

CUSTOMER SERVICE CONCEPT

No discussion of the communication tools available to librarians would be complete without mention of total quality management (TQM) and its focus on customer service. TQM became the byword in the 1980s and early 1990s for hundreds of companies and organizations whose intent is to serve customers. Jo Bell Whitlatch, in an article about customer service, indicates that there is no universal set of TQM principles but provides a composite listing.

1. Focus on the customer

2. Quality work the first time

3. Strategic holistic approach to improvement

4. Continuous improvement as a way of life

5. Mutual respect and teamwork[27]

Customer satisfaction is germane to all other concepts within TQM, and all processes, policies, and procedures are designed to enhance that satisfaction. TQM can be approached in two generic ways: via a customer-handling approach, emphasizing the development and improvement of communication skills of service personnel; or with the blueprinting approach, which looks at the inadequacies and problems of the service-delivery system.[28]

For libraries operating in the nonprofit, public environment, there are some difficulties with implementing TQM to the fullest extent.

First, in the public sector the conflict between the program's direct customers (immediate users) and its ultimate customers (general public; taxpayers) can be acute: General taxpayers may prefer to minimize costs while direct customers may expect a level of quality found only at a very high cost. Second, the focus on customer needs and wants may be less effective in the rapidly changing high technology environment of library reference services.[29]

TQM was developed for the for-profit business. It evaluates success by sales or income figures. Front-line personnel are to be empowered, but library employees may be hampered by externally imposed guidelines. In libraries, policies that cause customer dissatisfaction may not be changeable (overdue fines, unattended children). "The fact that the literature is not tailor-made for us [libraries] does not mean we should give up and be satisfied with the way we do things now. Librarians should only be wary of adopting for-profit customer services in environments where they don't fit well."[30]

Along with the concept of TQM have been developed a wide range of training materials that are now available to enhance any customer service program. Videos, audiotapes, workbooks, study guides, and other materials are readily available from a variety of sources. "When reading about, listening to or viewing examples of good customer service, the message is generally the same: 'Successful customer service connects customers to what they need, but also leaves them satisfied and happy. The best interactions make customers eager to return.' "[31]

For the most part, training materials for customer service cover many of the same verbal and nonverbal skills already mentioned in this chapter; thus, they can be useful as an adjunct to any library service program.

FOLLOW-UP

The actual reference interview can be a complex dialogue that requires effective communication skills, but what follows an interview may be even more complex. During the course of actually doing reference work, a variety of things happen that may require the reference staff to take further steps after the patron is gone.

For example, the longer a reference librarian works with a particular collection of materials, the more obvious any gaps in the collection will become. As patrons ask for information about a subject, reference librarians will be the first to realize that the collection is inadequate to meet such information requests. Perhaps the library has no materials, or they are outdated or in insufficient numbers.

Therefore, the collection development nature of reference service is critical. Reference librarians who can identify crucial gaps in reference, periodical, and circulating collections (book and nonbook), databases, and CD-ROMs should work to see that those gaps are filled. In a small library operation, this may be a relatively easy task, with little red tape hindering the effort. Budget considerations are usually the greatest obstacle to filling in gaps quickly. The larger the library organization, however, the more difficult it becomes to expedite orders. Acquisitions departments may have specific guidelines for what is a rush order, or perhaps only collection development librarians may originate orders. Whatever the system, reference librarians should try to use the existing system or create a procedure by which gaps in the collection can be filled in a reasonable amount of time.

REFERENCE LIBRARIAN AS INTERMEDIARY

Intermediary, *ombudsman*, and *troubleshooter* are all words that can be applied to a reference librarian. Librarians are intermediaries not only between the patron and the library, but often between the patron and the library departments as well. The extent to which a reference librarian is successful in this role depends on the general philosophy of service upon which the library operates. If public services and technical services view their roles differently, acting as a troubleshooter or intermediary becomes a delicate operation.

The following are a few examples of situations that arise in libraries when the reference staff might feel the need to be intermediaries:

- Patron needs an item that is being cataloged, is being prepared for the bindery, or is being repaired.[32]
- Patron needs an interlibrary loan.
- Patron needs an online search.
- Patrons are consistently confused by the building.
- Librarian working with a patron finds errors in local databases or catalog.
- Patron asks about a fine, overdue material, or getting a library card.
- Patron is upset over treatment in another part of the library or has a complaint about the library.
- Patron complains about equipment failures.
- Patron is frustrated by having to use several branch libraries.

Reference librarians may also find themselves having to do follow-up when dealing with patrons who are students. This can be in a school or public setting. Rather than continuing to cope term after term with unclear class assignments, library scavenger hunts, or the same specific fact question, the librarian may want to call upon the instructor. This is an opportunity for the librarian to suggest clarification of an assignment or library instruction of some kind. When reference librarians do library instruction as well, there is no need to make a referral to a bibliographic instruction librarian or department. If the librarian approaches an instructor with the attitude that the main concern is having students learn, the follow-up will generally not be viewed negatively. Some teachers, however, cannot be convinced that any modification or instruction is necessary, and the librarian will just have to accept it.

HANDLING COMPLAINTS

There will be times when it seems that all patrons have problems and frustrations, which they are taking to the reference librarian in desperation. The patron who needs another service of the library is generally the easiest to handle, usually with an efficient referral to the appropriate staff member. A reticent patron, however, may be intimidated by being sent off to another department, especially in a large library. A quick call ahead to the appropriate department can alert the staff to watch for the patron and help with the information need. In library settings where service to patrons is a high priority, reference librarians feel no qualms about sending a patron to a cataloger, a serials librarian, or an online searcher, knowing that the patron will receive courteous, competent service. In some libraries, patrons are discouraged from going into "nonpublic" areas, and the public service staff are expected to act officially on the patron's behalf.

Arlene Sirkin asserts that libraries usually do not have a complaint system, or the one that exists is underutilized. Often just listening sympathetically and explaining the situation and why the library cannot resolve the problem right away is enough.[33]

Patrons with complaints may want a variety of responses from the library staff.

- To be taken seriously
- To be treated with respect
- To get immediate action
- To clear up a problem so it never happens again
- To be listened to[34]

There are some specific techniques that can be used in handling complaints, and they dovetail with all the basic skills already mentioned. The librarian must understand what the "real" complaint is. By listening for the facts, acknowledging the patron's concern, allowing the patron to describe the complaint fully, and clarifying what the patron expects the librarian to do will keep the conversation focused and fact-based rather than emotional. In resolving the complaint, if possible, explain what the patron can expect, suggest what the patron can do to help, and thank the patron for reporting the problem.[35]

When faced with a patron who continues with a complaint, use the *broken record technique* rather than arguing or bargaining. Using the technique, keep emphasizing your point (e.g., "We close at 5 p.m. every Friday because so few people come to the library on Friday evenings") again and again.[36] If a complaint is beyond the librarian's control and it is possible to do so, the patron should be referred to a supervisor or someone else who is in a better position to assist.

Confusion about a particular library building is quite apparent to a reference librarian who is new to a situation. As a user of the buildings, a new reference librarian faces the same problems as the patrons. Unclear or outdated signs, lack of signs, or departments and offices that are not clearly labeled can all cause unnecessary delays, require detailed instructions, and generate endless questions. Reference librarians can suggest signs, changes, and the like in an effort to help all users.

Dealing with user complaints is difficult and requires a great deal of tact and patience. When possible, complaints should be channeled to the appropriate person. Arguing, going on the defensive, or insulting a patron will not help the situation. Listening skills are crucial during a complaint. What may become apparent upon close listening is that the patron has had a bad day or a bad experience elsewhere and is now venting frustration. Listen closely and try to discern the true nature of the complaint. Nonverbal behaviors, such as good eye contact, should be attentive and positive. Tone of voice should remain calm. When the patron has a legitimate complaint, the librarian should empathize with the patron's feelings of frustration. When the complaint is about another staff member, the librarian should be tactful and professional. "In these instances, it is important to avoid putting one's colleagues in another unit on the defensive or deprecating another unit to a patron."[37] Professional differences should be settled behind the scenes.

Librarians should be particularly wary of complaints about items in the collection. Never argue the moral, religious, or political merits of library materials when facing a patron who wants something immediately withdrawn. Every library should have a written policy on handling such complaints, but many do not. When no formal or informal policy is available, the patron should be asked to put the complaint in writing. The majority of complaints of this nature fade away when something must be put on paper. Here again, the reference librarian should remain calm and professional throughout the conversation. As with all complaints, the most important interview skills are eye contact, relaxed posturing, facial expression, and tone of voice that reflect the *mood* of the user (which does not necessarily imply agreement with the complaint).

In conclusion, even when the reference interview is successfully completed, it may require a number of follow-up measures from the reference staff. An important point to remember is that if you promise to contact the patron after an answer or solution is found, it is critical that you do so. Almost nothing makes a worse impression than the promise of further assistance without the delivery of help. The most important result of follow-up should be providing a procedure, policy, or solution in anticipation of the next time the situation occurs. No matter how much in-house work and communication has taken place, the need of the user should always be kept in mind.

NOTES

[1]Patricia Dewdney and Catherine Sheldrick Ross, "Flying a Light Aircraft: Reference Service Evaluation from a User's Viewpoint," *RQ* 34 (winter 1994): 218.

[2]Ibid., 219.

[3]Allen E. Ivey, *Microcounseling: Innovations in Interviewing Training* (Springfield, IL: Thomas, 1971).

[4]Elaine Zaremba Jennerich, "Microcounseling in Library Education" (Ph.D. diss., University of Pittsburgh, 1974).

[5]Edward J. Jennerich and Elaine Z. Jennerich, "Teaching the Reference Interview," *Journal of Education for Librarianship* 17 (fall 1976): 106–11.

[6]Ivey, *Microcounseling: Innovations in Interviewing Training*; Allen E. Ivey and Jerry Anthier, *Microcounseling: Innovations in Interviewing, Counseling, Psychotherapy, and Psychoeducation* (Springfield, IL: Thomas, 1978).

[7]Allen E. Ivey, Norma B. Gluckstern, and Mary Bradford Ivey, *Basic Attending Skills,* 3d ed. (North Amherst, MA: Microtraining Associates, 1992), 131.

[8]Barbara Conroy and Barbara Schindler Jones, *Improving Communication in the Library* (Phoenix, AZ: Oryx Press, 1986), 120.

[9]Ibid., 121.

[10]Edward T. Hall, *The Silent Language* (Garden City, NY: Doubleday, 1959).

[11]Chris L. Kleinke, *First Impressions: The Psychology of Encountering Others* (Englewood Cliffs, NJ: Prentice Hall, 1975).

[12]Julius Fast, *Body Language* (New York: Pocket Books, 1982).

[13]Conroy and Jones, *Improving Communication,* 114.

[14]Catherine Sheldrick Ross and Patricia Dewdney. *Communicating Professionally: A How-to-Do-It Manual for Library Applications* (New York: Neal-Schuman, 1989), 147.

[15]Ibid., 25–46.

[16]Christopher Nolan, "Closing the Reference Interview: Implications for Policy and Practice," *RQ* 31 (summer 1992): 520.

[17]Reference and Adult Services Division, American Library Association, "Guidelines for Medical, Legal, and Business Responses at General Reference Desks," *RQ* 31 (summer 1992): 554–55.

[18]Catherine Sheldrick Ross, "How to Find Out What People Really Want to Know," *Reference Librarian* 16 (winter 1986): 27.

[19]Vicky L. Crosson, "Hey! Kids Are Patrons, Too!" *Texas Libraries* 52 (summer 1991): 48–50.

[20]Ross and Dewdney, *Communicating Professionally,* 25–46.

[21]Geraldine B. King, "Open and Closed Questions: The Reference Interview," *RQ* 12 (winter 1972): 158.

[22]Marilyn J. Markham, Keith H. Stirling, and Nathan M. Smith, "Librarian Self-Disclosure and Patron Satisfaction in the Reference Interview," *RQ* 22 (spring 1983): 371.

[23]Brenda Dervin and Patricia Dewdney, "Neutral Questioning: A New Approach to the Reference Interview," *RQ* 25 (summer 1986): 508–9.

[24]Ibid., 506–13.

[25]Ross, "How to Find Out," 19–30.

[26]Ross and Dewdney, *Communicating Professionally.*

[27]Jo Bell Whitlatch, "Customer Service: Implications for Reference Practice," *Reference Librarian,* no. 49/50 (1995): 9.

[28]Gwen Arthur, "Customer-Service Training in Academic Libraries," *Journal of Academic Librarianship* 20 (September 1994): 222.

[29]Whitlatch, "Customer Service," 10.

[30]Julie Beth Todaro, "Make 'Em Smile," *School Library Journal* 41 (January 1995): 25.

[31]Ibid., 25.

[32]Diana M. Thomas, Ann T. Hinckley, and Elizabeth R. Eisenbach, *The Effective Reference Librarian* (New York: Academic Press, 1981), 24.

[33]Arlene Farber Sirkin, "Implementing a Total Quality Management Program." *Journal of Library Administration* 18, no. 1/2 (1993): 77–78.

[34]Rebecca L. Morgan, *Calming Upset Customers: Staying Effective During Unpleasant Situations* (Menlo Park, CA: Crisp Publications, 1989), 36.

[35]Ross and Dewdney, *Communicating Professionally,* 127–29.

[36]Ibid., 129.

[37]Thomas, Hinckley, and Eisenbach, *Effective Reference Librarian,* 25.

3

Teaching the Role

It is readily apparent from the literature discussed in the previous chapters that the concept of the reference interview has been clearly established over a long period of time within the library profession. The work of Flexner, Maxfield, Taylor, Jennerich, Dewdney, and others clearly demonstrates that there is an ample body of scholarly knowledge available to the profession which deals with the reference interview process.

THE NEED TO TEACH INTERVIEWING

Of course, arguments can be made that there are many good reference librarians who have not undergone an education program emphasizing reference interviewing techniques. This is a high compliment indeed, both to the profession and to those individuals. However, what concerns the authors is the present lack of any systematized methodology for ensuring that students who become professional librarians are competent in interviewing skills. The existing education system assumes that a student, by being knowledgeable about collections and technology, will become a good reference librarian. This is not always the case. The converse is also true; that is, someone who is good at reference interviewing techniques but does not know reference tools will be pleasant but not terribly effective. What is needed is someone who is able to determine the client's information needs effectively and then to satisfy those needs using the myriad tools of the library. This ideal cannot be achieved with any assurance by simply teaching students to know reference sources. The library profession and the library education community have the responsibility to train students to be competent both in knowledge of sources and technology and in interviewing skills. In an era of assessment and quality control, the library education community cannot ignore its responsibility to train practioners in more effective communication techniques.

Although the format of information sources is changing rapidly, the necessity for competence in reference interviewing skills has not diminished. Indeed, the need for good reference interviewing skills will increase as the number and formats of materials increase. Time is money, particularly in an online environment where time spent can result in substantial charges. It is increasingly important for the reference librarian to conduct a thorough reference interview before going to any sources.

In one of the first conferences devoted entirely to the reference interview, sponsored by the Canadian Library Association in 1977, faculty from Magill University reported on teaching the interview. Dishearteningly, however, one of the papers indicated that although the reference interview must be learned, it could not really be taught.[1] The overall conclusion was that there is a need to analyze and discuss the interview throughout the profession.

At Brigham Young University's graduate library school, Nathan Smith and others worked to introduce the interview directly into the curriculum and to have students learn the necessary skills.[2] Gerald Jahoda,[3] Jovian Lange,[4] and Bernard Lukenbill[5] have also discussed ways in which communication skills should be integrated into the curriculum. Other educators, such as Charles Patterson[6] and Margaret Steig,[7] warn that too much emphasis on communication skills and not enough on knowledge of books and other sources can also be detrimental to producing well-rounded reference professionals.

Fortunately, more attention is now being paid to teaching the reference interview in library schools. Often this is because a particular faculty member has a positive, dynamic interest in the subject, rather than because a criterion has been systematically introduced into the curriculum. Automated resources have also emphasized the need for interviewing techniques, as librarians realize that mediated online searches require an effective and well-focused interview.

A look at library school catalogs reveals that the *process* of reference, as well as the sources, is often now included in the curriculum. For example, fundamentals of the reference interview are included in the courses at Simmons College, San Jose State, Rosary College, University of Washington, Kent State University, Clark Atlanta University, University of Hawaii, and University of Wisconsin-Milwaukee, to name a few. Other library schools include topics such as skills in question negotiation, techniques in reference transactions, or philosophy and components of quality reference service. Future librarians should learn not only the resources and materials, but also the *process* of reference service, including the interview. Both are critical in the training and functioning of librarians, and neither should be emphasized to the detriment of the other.

TEACHING TECHNIQUES

An extremely successful attempt to incorporate both content and process into the teaching of reference was undertaken at Baylor University during the years 1974 to 1983. The approach used was based on microcounseling techniques, originally developed by Allen Ivey and adapted specifically for library school students by Elaine Jennerich. The course, "Basic Reference," was available to students enrolled in the undergraduate program for learning resources specialists taught by Edward Jennerich. Students were first given a basic introduction to the philosophy and parameters of reference services within the totality of library operations. The second component of the course was an introduction to the verbal and nonverbal communication skills that students would be using throughout the semester. The third component of the course was discussion and study of reference materials.

The course was taught in a fairly traditional manner, beginning with general reference works and proceeding to more specialized reference works within specific academic disciplines. What distinguished the method used in this course was the total inclusion of reference interview techniques within the framework of a traditional course. Students were not only given assignments to study and take extensive notes on reference works, but were also assigned specific reference question problems to answer using those references.

In addition, the students were required to role-play in reference interview situations. For this exercise, the physical arrangement of the classroom was important. The classroom/laboratory was constructed in a large room in the basement of the university library. The room contained a large seminar desk where the class itself was taught and which housed a small, representative collection of reference books. Approximately one-third of the existing classroom was partitioned off with a one-way glass mirror. This viewing room was used by the class to observe the practice reference interview sessions. Behind the glass partition, videotape equipment recorded the various reference interviews. The videotape camera had a powerful zoom lens that allowed close observation of student facial expressions and eye contact. In addition to the camera, the microphone for the videotape equipment was hung inconspicuously from the ceiling of the classroom, with the wire running above the ceiling tiles back to the videotape equipment. This enabled the class to observe and hear what was transpiring in the reference classroom.

Students were required to participate in the reference interview sessions, which were held once a week. At the beginning of class, a student was randomly selected to play the role of the reference librarian. The remainder of the class then role-played library patrons. Each of these mock reference interviews lasted approximately 20 minutes. While the reference librarian was working in the reference collection, students were randomly sent into the "library" to ask the reference librarian questions that the students had previously developed. The only limits on the questions were (1) that the answer be logically locatable in one of the reference books in the practice reference collection, and (2) that the answer reasonably be expected to be found in the materials covered in class up to that time. This point should be emphasized: The reference interview process was cumulative over the course of the semester, requiring aptitude and knowledge of the reference books covered up to that point.

As the "patron" approached the reference librarian and asked the question, the instructor and the rest of the class observed from behind the glass partition. The reference interview was videotaped and discussed by the entire class later in the class period. At the beginning of the semester, the practicing reference librarians generally dealt with one patron at a time, to gain facility and confidence in the process. As the semester progressed, the pace of new patrons coming into the library was staggered and increased to create a more realistic situation. Therefore, at various times there were one, two, three, and even four people waiting to have a reference question answered by the reference librarian. To add realism to the process, a telephone that could be activated by the instructor was installed in the classroom. So, in addition to live patrons, there was also the ever-present, ringing telephone.

EVALUATING THE INTERVIEWERS

Each student was videotaped for approximately 20 minutes. Generally, in the course of an hour-and-a-half class, three students could be videotaped as reference librarians. After three students role-played as reference librarians, the remainder of the class and the instructor evaluated each "reference librarian" using a specially developed rating sheet (see table 3-1) based on the 12 verbal and nonverbal communication skills discussed in chapter 2. Various perceptions, questions, comments, and so on were discussed by the peer group, guided by the instructor.

Frequently there were varying perceptions as to what actually occurred or whether a particular open question was effective or appropriate, and so forth. At this point, the videotape was played back and analyzed in detail by the class and the practice reference librarian. This was often a fascinating exercise, as what was perceived to have occurred frequently had not. Guidance and suggestions were given by the instructor at the end of each student's session. The rating sheets were given to the student reference librarian for review and reflection. The videotapes were saved by the instructor for the entire semester, and students had the opportunity to review their own videotapes at any point during the course of the semester. Depending upon the size of the class in any given semester, each student enrolled in the course generally had three or four individual turns as reference librarian.

At the end of the semester, the instructor reviewed the videotapes and the rating forms for each student. A grade was assigned for the reference interview portion, which counted for 40 percent of the grade for the course.

Table 3.1. Interviewing Rating Sheet

	EXCEL.	GOOD	AVER.	FAIR	POOR	NOTO*
1. Eye Contact						
2. Gestures						
3. Posture						
4. Facial Expression/Tone of Voice						
5. Remembering						
6. Avoiding Premature Diagnosis						
7. Reflecting Feelings Verbally						
8. Restating or Paraphrasing Contents						
9. Using Encouragers						
10. Closing						
11. Giving Opinions/Suggestions						
12. Asking Open Questions						
*No opportunity to observe						

Source: *Journal of Education for Librarianship* 17, no. 2 (fall 1976): 108. Reprinted by permission.

Generally speaking, student attitudes toward the process were overwhelmingly favorable. However, this was not always the perception of the process at the beginning of the semester. Students naturally had fears about being videotaped, about role-playing in general, and about being able to complete the course requirements. However, as the course progressed, the students became comfortable with the process and frequently forgot that they were being videotaped or role-playing. Of the more than 200 students taught in the span of nine years, only one had a serious problem with the role-playing situation. The instructor and the student discussed this at length, and the student was encouraged to attempt to conduct the reference interviews. Though experiencing great trepidation initially, the student eventually became so involved with answering the reference questions that she forgot she was being videotaped, and the problem resolved itself. This example illustrates the importance of the instructor's presenting a positive attitude toward the procedure and thoroughly explaining its value. Failure to do so may result in student hostility toward both the professor and the process.

Student criticism concerning the course noted that the videotaping, the use of class peers, and the methodology used in the small reference collection lent a sense of artificiality to the process. To eliminate this element, students were assigned to work at the university reference desk under the supervision of the university librarians. This process could not have been undertaken without the complete support and cooperation of the university reference staff. The students found this to be an extremely valuable part of the learning experience, and the university librarians were grateful for the additional help. These assignments were generally undertaken after the midway point in the semester, when the students had become comfortable with the basic reference sources and the basic concept of the reference interviewing process.

Judging by the evaluations, the technique used in teaching the reference course was overwhelmingly successful. All the students who participated in the process showed improvement over the course of the semester, as indicated on the rating forms completed by students and the professor. Evidence also indicated that once students had completed the course and became professional librarians, they maintained their reference interview skills. This conclusion is based upon conversations with their supervisors and with the librarians themselves. There did not seem to be any loss of knowledge of reference materials and basic bibliography. Additionally, students were able to integrate their reference interview skills with reference book content knowledge and thus provide better service to library patrons. This is the primary aim of incorporating reference interviewing into reference courses.

There was no apparent distraction in the teaching/learning process from the use of the videotape equipment. The fact that the equipment was behind a one-way glass mirror kept it out of the immediate view of the student who was role-playing, and thus it did not hinder the teaching situation. Likewise, not staring at a camera quickly put the students at ease, and they were able to concentrate on developing their interviewing skills and on using the reference materials in the practice collection properly.

The method of instruction outlined here has successfully proven that microcounseling and reference interviewing techniques can be used effectively in the training of librarians, while at the same time developing their knowledge of reference materials. This will result in improved service to library patrons— which is, after all, the reason for the existence of the profession of librarianship.

The concept of the microskills training model is also espoused by Catherine Sheldrick Ross and Patricia Dewdney in their book *Communicating Professionally*.[8] Using Allen Ivey's microtraining concept, they outline steps that can be taken to develop training for the reference interview. Unlike the Jennerichs' controlled experiment, which taught a number of verbal and nonverbal skills at the same time, Ross and Dewdney interpreted Ivey's concept very strictly to teach one skill at a time.[9] By focusing on only one skill at a time, both trainer and trainee isolate that skill and can concentrate on it more effectively.

Five steps for training sessions are:

- Define the skill. Discuss with the trainee the value of the skill, what it is, and how it can be used in a library setting.

- Demonstrate the skill. This can be accomplished with audio, video, role-playing, or other methods.

- Read about the skill from books, articles, or handouts.

- Practice the skill through supervised exercises or role-playing.

- Assess. Trainees should practice a skill on the job or in another situation and assess how using the skill worked or did not work.[10]

Having trainees (library school students or working librarians/staff) videotaped so they can observe their behavior is often intimidating and can cause anxiety. There are a number of ways to reduce this anxiety. Subjects should know the purpose of the tapes and how the tapes will be used. Subjects can view their own tapes privately, and only volunteers would have theirs viewed by a group. In assessing videos, a trainer should always concentrate on what is being done right rather than wrong. For example, it is better to say, "She restated the patron's need several times during the interview" rather than, "She didn't ask any open questions."

Audiotape recording was used in a field experiment meant to be a controlled inquiry into the effects of training librarians in the skills of the reference interview in a natural setting. Dewdney compared two training models. One training method taught librarians neutral questioning. Participants learned the use of neutral questions as well as the use of open questions and avoidance of premature diagnosis. The second model taught librarians five microskills, including restatement, use of encouragers, open questioning, closure, and avoidance of premature diagnosis. The third method was a control group in which librarians had group discussions about reference interviews but received no specific skills training. Librarians were taped doing actual interviews using a wireless microphone and a small transmitter. Content analysis was performed on the interviews.

The findings support the positive effect of training for specific skills:

> [P]rocedures revealed statistically significant differences between training types with the posttraining period and between the pretraining and posttraining skill levels for the two structured training groups but not for the control group. . . . Although the median level of skills increased for all three groups, more significant changes occurred for librarians trained in neutral questioning, in that they demonstrated increased levels of skill in avoiding premature diagnosis, asking open questions, and asking neutral questions. . . . Librarians trained in microskills showed significant increases in the use of open questions, but not, surprisingly, in the use of other skills.[11]

NOTES

[1]Peter F. McNally, "Teaching and Learning the Reference Interview," in *The Reference Interview: Proceedings of the CACUL Symposium on the Reference Interview of the Annual Conference of the Canadian Library Association*, ed. Elizabeth Silvester and Lillian Rider (Montreal: Canadian Library Association, 1977), 69–81.

[2]Nathan M. Smith and Steven D. Fitt, "Active Listening at the Reference Desk," *RQ* 21 (spring 1982): 247–49; Nathan M. Smith and G. Hugh Allred, "Recognizing and Coping with the Vertical Patron," *Special Libraries* 67 (November 1976): 528–33; Mark J. Thompson, Nathan M. Smith, and Bonnie L. Woods, "A Proposed Model of Self-Disclosure," *RQ* 20 (winter 1980): 160–64.

[3]Gerald Jahoda, "Some Unanswered Questions," *Reference Librarian*, no. 1/2 (fall/winter 1981): 159.

[4]Fr. Jovian Lange, "The Great Joy," *Reference Librarian*, no. 1/2 (fall/winter 1981): 163.

[5]W. Bernard Lukenbill, "Teaching Helping Relationship Concepts in the Reference Process," *Journal of Education for Librarianship* 18 (fall 1977): 110–20.

[6]Charles D. Patterson, "Books Remain Basic," *Reference Librarian*, no. 1/2 (fall/winter 1981): 171–72.

[7]Margaret Steig, "In Defense of Problems: The Classical Method of Teaching," *Journal of Education for Librarianship* 20 (winter 1980): 171–83.

[8]Catherine Sheldrick Ross and Patricia Dewdney, *Communicating Professionally: A How-to-Do-It Manual for Library Applications* (New York: Neal-Schuman, 1989), 264.

[9]Ibid., 264.

[10]Ibid., 264–65.

[11]Patricia Dewdney, "Recording the Reference Interview: A Field Experiment," in *Qualitative Research in Information Management,* ed. Jack D. Glazier and Ronald R. Powell (Englewood, CO: Libraries Unlimited, 1992), 134.

4

CASTING

This chapter discusses various traits, generally intangible, that may be needed to become a successful reference librarian—or, to be more precise, the traits that may be needed to conduct a successful interview. The chapter also covers the importance and role of paraprofessionals and student assistants in the provision of reference service.

CHARACTERISTICS OF REFERENCE LIBRARIANS

Each practicing reference librarian, administrator, and library school faculty member probably has a different set of traits that each feels makes the ideal reference librarian. Technical services staff, patrons, and others may name yet another set of traits. There are, however, certain universal characteristics. Some of these traits can be learned on the job, but many are developed early in life and are adapted to a particular chosen career. Some of these characteristics are discussed in relation to the interview itself.

There is not total agreement as to what makes a good reference librarian. Various authors have approached the subject either in generalities or specifics. Charles Patterson, in an article entitled "Personality, Knowledge, and the Reference Librarian," sums up several articles by listing a number of important traits, including good memory, thoroughness, orderliness, accuracy, imagination, inquisitive mind, logical mind, outgoing personality, ability to interact, and a desire to help people.[1]

A characteristic often missing from many lists is a *sense of humor*—a quality definitely needed by a good reference librarian. Of all the possible traits to discuss, why does this come first? Librarianship, by its very nature, is consumed by details. If it isn't the abbreviations in an index entry, it is the directions on the photocopy machine or search strategies for a specialized database. Every day reference librarians are inundated with the details of the system, their own particular institution's peculiarities, and the flood of information from publishers, database vendors, the Internet, the World Wide Web, and the like. It is no wonder that librarians are so buried in detail they take themselves much too seriously or that patrons become frustrated. Yes, the business of providing accurate information in a timely manner is certainly important, but it should also be a joy.

Although a patron's inquiry may be serious in nature, and should be handled as such, there is no reason not to interject humor into the reference interview. Humor relieves stress, can allay anxiety (at least for a few moments), and relaxes everyone. However, humor should never be used to ridicule the patron or to make fun of colleagues or other patrons. Instead, it should be directed at oneself (not deprecatingly so), the system, or the situation. Children love humor and the use of it with them makes the librarian seem a bit more human and approachable. When dealing with people and the intricacies of a library, there are often opportunities to use humor, and those opportunities should be used to advantage. Thus, a good reference librarian should have a sense of humor. A librarian can be adequate at reference work without it, but the librarian who is adept at interviewing will always have a sense of humor.

Nancy Osborne surveyed a sample of librarians "to determine the frequency of their use of humor at the reference desk and in the library instruction classroom, their perceptions of classroom humor, and their reasons for using humor in these situations."[2] The two reasons librarians cited most often for using humor were to put the patron (or students) at ease and to establish rapport. As one librarian in the study remarked, "I believe that virtually any service-based interaction is enhanced by a sharing of smiles and/or humor. Shared humor creates a bond and the information transaction is then more likely to be a shared experience."[3]

Another trait a reference librarian should possess is *dedication* or *commitment*. This dedication should be to the profession as a whole, and more specifically to meeting the needs of patrons in their quests for information. A librarian who is dedicated to reference librarianship will automatically want to improve basic skills whenever possible. That dedication will also manifest itself in other ways. The dedicated librarian will go out of the way to help a patron, to follow up on an inquiry, or to try to change a policy that in some way thwarts the free flow of information or easy access to it. Almost evangelistic in their zeal, dedicated reference librarians must sometimes pull back and let the patron learn to help himself or herself. Perhaps such commitment comes from having chosen exactly the right profession or from being in a setting that motivates and rewards dedication. Whatever combination of factors engenders the dedication, it will be readily apparent to patrons. The patron who is a regular library user soon recognizes and appreciates that dedication and commitment. However, for the patron who works with a librarian only once, it may not be immediately apparent.

A *genuine liking for people* is another important trait. There is no way to conduct a successful interview without liking people. Such a person accepts people as they are, seldom makes assumptions about people without the facts, and enjoys the give-and-take of human interaction. Librarianship is one of the least isolated of professions. Many librarians do not have offices, so not only do they work with patrons a great deal, but they are also among people almost all the hours of their working lives. This does not mean that a successful reference librarian must have an effusive personality. Liking people has little to do with any particular approach, but it does convey to others an interest in them as individuals, not just as information seekers.

The literature of the profession often mentions *good memory* as being necessary for reference librarians. S. D. Neill defines three types of memory—semantic, episodic, and schematic—that contribute to the success of reference library interactions.[4] Sometimes the case can be overstated. Librarians without good memories are often able to use various devices to remember things. Actually, memory is fine as storage capacity, but quick recall of relevant items is even more important. During the interview, it is important to recall what the patron said and to summarize the patron's needs and adapt them to the library's system. Every librarian, faced with a busy reference day, will have trouble concentrating. Loss of concentration is the biggest deterrent to memory during the interview. One way to circumvent the problem is to jot down pertinent words or dates while the patron is talking to avoid the risk of having to ask the patron to repeat things. This technique is particularly useful when a librarian has no knowledge of the subject. For example, a patron might ask about the starch amylase, or the novelist, Eliza Haywood—and the librarian has never heard of either. Jot down the name (with correct spelling if the patron knows it). The paper can even be carried as the interview is continued as a reminder. If writing down such things during the interview is not thought of as a crutch, but rather as a memory device, the technique can be used confidently during the interview. No matter how good a memory a librarian has, he or she must listen to the patron carefully so what is remembered is accurate. Nothing is more irritating to a patron than sensing that the librarian may be hearing but not really listening.

Imagination and *creativity* are intangible traits that are helpful to a librarian during an interview. Thinking of imaginative open questions, encouragers, or ways to reflect feelings can make the encounter more interesting and productive. Another description of this trait is the ability to "think on your feet" to keep the communication loop open in helpful ways.

Patience and *persistence* go hand in hand to make a librarian more successful during the interview. Even though the librarian may be talking to the eighth or ninth student asking about the same thing, the librarian must be patient during the interview. Patience pays off, particularly when the librarian is patient enough to conduct an interview that reveals that the ninth student is asking about something totally unrelated after all. It is all too easy to get lulled into complacency or preassessment of a question during term-paper or class project times of the year. Persistence, of course, is needed in pursuing answers, but it also pays off during interviews with shy, reticent, or recalcitrant patrons.

Among the list of desirable traits, *energy* and *stamina* must be added. Dealing with people and the system, while exhilarating and challenging, can also be exhausting. High energy levels are needed to conduct interview after interview at a busy service point. If a librarian has developed good rapport, it doesn't matter if he or she is "on duty." Patrons will ask for or seek the librarian out. Such patron behavior is high praise, but constant patron contact, not to mention other staff contact, is demanding. Without a high energy level and stamina, it is difficult to keep performance levels up to standards. It is amusing that some people assume librarians have lots of time to read because they work in such a quiet, peaceful setting.

The ability to jump quickly from one subject to another is important for the general reference librarian, but what about the specialist? Even in a medical or business library, the possibilities of numerous topics arising in the course of one day are high. In Neill's article, entitled "Problem Solving and the Reference Process," he states that reference librarians should have a preference for the ambiguous and the unexpected.[5] Reference interviews, in fact, can be thought of as exercises in clarifying ambiguities. It never even occurs to the effective reference librarian to be nervous or afraid about what the next question might be or what the next patron will be like. Obviously this is not true the first time a librarian works at a new job, though.

Service orientation was studied by Gillian and Bryce Allen as a selection criterion for public services librarians. By analyzing job advertisements and comparing those with the selectors who were responsible for hiring, the researchers concluded that service orientation generally ranked first among selection criteria, even though it was not strongly stated in advertisements. Gillian and Bryce Allen believe that "the identification of job applicants with a high degree of Service Orientation would . . . be helpful in the identification of public service librarians who would be pleasant, tactful, and socially competent in their relations with others."[6]

Additional characteristics could also be mentioned, such as empathetic behavior, wide-ranging interests, and the like. Suffice it to say that librarianship has some idea of the kinds of general traits that are needed to be a good reference librarian. Further research into these traits, however, might help library science students choose one part of the profession over another. To date, little has been done in library preparation programs to assist students to select a particular facet of the profession. Rather, whether a student chooses to become a public service or technical service librarian is largely a matter of self-selection or the vagaries of the marketplace.

Though all of the interview skills discussed earlier can be learned, some students and librarians already possess many of these skills as products of their personalities, backgrounds, training, and socialization. A librarian, student, or staff member who already possesses many of the skills probably will not have to work too hard to refine them or add the other skills. In some cases, even though a student or librarian does not have the skills innately, the traits of commitment to service and willingness to learn will help them to master and adopt interviewing skills rather quickly. For the student or librarian who cannot understand the need for better communication, who shows no real empathy for others, and who approaches reference only in terms of physical resources, it may be difficult or almost impossible to learn interviewing skills, or even to want to.

The profession is far from agreeing upon the specific personality traits that make a good reference librarian. The study of the issue has begun, however, and, it is hoped, can be applied in a useful manner in the future.

SUPPORTING ROLES

Every librarian should understand the importance of paraprofessional, clerical, and student assistant staff to the smooth operation of a library. For purposes of discussion, we use the term *paraprofessional* to mean anyone who works in a library who does not have an M.L.S. and *student assistant* to mean part-time student workers, pages, and interns who work in the library. In "A Commitment to Information Services," the RUSA guidelines state that "A professional librarian/ information specialist should be available to users during all hours the library is open."[7] Although many libraries strive to attain that goal, most libraries are unable to meet such demands. In public libraries, a paraprofessional is generally in charge of public services when a professional is not available, but many academic libraries sometimes leave the facility in the care of student assistants, particularly during late night or weekend hours.

The dispute over whether paraprofessionals and student assistants can perform reference work well will continue for many years to come. In reality, most paraprofessionals will do some reference work, and some student assistants will perform public service tasks. No matter what is said about paraprofessionals, two things should be borne in mind. First, on-the-job training is *not* equivalent to a degree in library science. Such training by its very nature suffers time and subject-depth constraints that cannot be avoided. Even when, as some research has indicated, paraprofessionals do well conducting interviews, they do not do as well as professionals across the board on *all* types of questions.[8] In a study reported in 1988, paraprofessionals and librarians were rated by library patrons.[9] The conclusions supported the argument that paraprofessionals have more communication difficulty and more difficulty negotiating reference queries than do professional librarians.

Second, no matter what training one receives, there are simply people who do not deal well with the public, who are not particularly interested in helping others, and who may, in fact, be rather unpleasant with patrons at the least sign of stress. Some paraprofessionals and students are by temperament and personality unsuited to the demands of continuous public service work.

PARAPROFESSIONALS

All types of libraries use paraprofessional staff to answer patron inquiries. Paraprofessionals are often in charge of reference areas, or indeed, of entire libraries in many different settings for varying amounts of time. The extent to which a paraprofessional can be entrusted with the task of performing reference work is a complex issue. Of primary importance to remember is that "it is not the library's intent to slowly transform non-professionals into librarians." [10] Also, some paraprofessionals are more suited to reference work than others. Among the factors to be taken into consideration when choosing which parapro- fessionals should receive some reference instruction are

- Educational level

- Motivation

- Genuine liking for people

- Willingness to learn

Julie McDaniel and Judith Ohles, in *Training Paraprofessionals for Reference Service*, summarize the arguments for and against using paraprofessionals for reference service. McDaniel and Ohles's reasons for using paraprofessionals include:

- Directional and ready reference questions can be answered well by paraprofessionals.

- Libraries can offer individual assistance to patrons and possibly increase the number of service hours.

- Paraprofessionals with subject specialties can augment the reference librarian's knowledge.

Arguments against using paraprofessionals include:

- Paraprofessionals may not be able to recognize the need for or conduct reference interviews.

- Incorrect referrals can be made by paraprofessionals, or, in their eagerness to serve, they may answer questions incorrectly.

- A great deal of time is expended in training and supervising parapro- fessionals.

- High turnover, particularly of those who have subject expertise, interrupts continuity. [11]

Of the many training programs for paraprofessionals reported in the litera- ture, the majority, like Kathleen Coleman and Elizabeth Magutti's "Training Nonprofessionals for Reference Service," concentrate on materials-based edu- cation. [12] For example, paraprofessionals must learn to handle and teach patrons about serials, printouts, and catalogs. Also, interpreting entries in various indexes, helping users to locate materials throughout the library or system, and using basic factual reference books can be part of the training. Such time-intensive training is important but all too often lacking in many libraries.

STUDENT ASSISTANTS

As a rule, public, special, and school libraries use students to work directly with the library's clientele generally on a limited basis. Academic libraries, in contrast, often use students in public service roles. In some cases, students are used exclusively for evening or weekend hours. The standards for college libraries are specific about discouraging this practice. "During the normal hours of operation the users deserve competent, professional service. The high value of the library's collections, associated materials, and equipment, etc., dictates that a responsible individual be in control at all times." [13]

Student assistants can be a big help to public service, but even though they should receive some training, a large investment in training time does not pay off in the same way as training for permanent full-time or part-time paraprofessionals. For students, the part-time library job is not the primary focus of their lives. Nevertheless, responsible students want to do a good job and can with some training. Those who are friendly, outgoing, and honest will help enhance the image of the library with its patrons. *Honest* is a key word because one of the more difficult things for beginning student assistants to do is admit "I don't know." Remember that these are people who are in academic classes, where saying "I don't know" may be admitting that an assignment was not completed, or admitting ignorance of a topic. So, when a student does not know the answer to a patron's question, he or she should be taught that there are several correct responses, all of which begin with "I don't know." For example:

- "I don't know, but I'll get someone else to help you."
- "I don't know, but let me call _____ to find out."
- "I don't know and, since I'm the only one here, I'll leave a message for a librarian to get back to you."

Obviously, there are many more variations, but students must understand that a guess is not an answer and that it is perfectly fine to admit they do not know something.

In *Training Student Library Assistants*, the authors discuss training students for one-on-one patron service. They suggest using videos or other training aids and pairing students who have experience in serving customers with those who do not. Among the rules of service suggested are:

- To the patron, you are the library. Maintain a positive public image.
- Service to patrons is the first priority.

- If you are sitting, get up and go to the patron.
- Smile and be polite.
- Listen attentively.
- Use your best judgment.[14]

Student assistants who are on duty should wear name tags. It is sometimes quite difficult to tell the difference between a beginning librarian and an upperclass student, particularly when the student is dressed "professionally." The tags do not have to have the student's name, but can say "Reference Student Assistant," "Library Student Assistant," "Student Assistant," or "Page." Students, particularly female students, generally prefer tags *without* their names. A tag accomplishes several things. First, it identifies a student as a member of the staff, which is helpful to patrons and, in large library settings, to other staff members. Also, the tags identify students as such, so they can feel better about saying "I don't know." In these instances it is important to let patrons know they are not dealing with a librarian.

The most important qualification for a student assistant is a positive and friendly attitude. The expectation of such an attitude should be stressed both in the hiring interview and in any orientation programs for students. Students should be expected to come to work alert and with a pleasant manner.

Student assistants also need some general orientation and instruction. The more complex and diversified the library system is, the more instruction students may need. Among the things students should know are

- How to use the telephone system
- Basic library computer systems
- Telephone etiquette and service
- Overview of library services and operations
- Names and faces of reference librarians and paraprofessionals
- Customer service philosophy
- Location of major divisions and offices in the library
- Emergency procedures
- Location of each type of collection in the library (e.g., reference, media, microforms, etc.)
- Reporting relationships
- Proper use of any equipment in reference

If students are to be left alone at a service location for long periods of time, reference librarians should decide exactly how much more training to give and to what extent they want students to try to answer reference questions. Additional training should include using online catalogs, interpreting entries, and the use of high-demand reference tools.

In terms of reference interviewing skills, training should concentrate on a limited number of skills. For student assistants, the most important skills are eye contact, facial expression, tone of voice, and remembering. Student assistants should understand that the patron should receive their full attention and eye contact as soon as the patron approaches them. An expression of sincerity, both facially and orally, is important. The one nonverbal behavior that is critical is remembering, and student assistants should be encouraged to listen carefully to patrons and to write things down.

There are several reasons why students must be encouraged to remember carefully what patron needs are. To provide an appropriate answer or referral, the student assistant must listen. Careful listening is also crucial when student assistants relate patron needs to a library staff member. Writing down key words, spellings, and the like may save time for a librarian later, but it is also good practice for a student assistant to further refine his or her listening skills. Trying to train even the best student assistants in the techniques of open questioning, reflecting feelings, or restating content goes beyond realistic expectations. If, in fact, all student assistants in the library who have any dealings with patrons are consistently using these four skills, the library is fortunate.

Simulation and role-playing are particularly useful tools for training student assistants. In *Training Student Library Assistants*, the authors suggest that "[s]tudents can be given an overview and hands-on instruction of a computerized system and practice with actual situations." [15]

The distinction between student assistants and professional librarians should be well defined, particularly to the public. The library's patrons should be aware that student assistants can offer only limited help. Obviously, name tags can help. Another method, described by Nancy Emmick in "Nonprofessionals on Reference Desks in Academic Libraries," is the development of signs displayed prominently at the reference area to alert patrons to the availability of service. [16] Table 4-1 on page 44 shows examples of such signs.

A better use of student assistant time is in assisting patrons with tasks that do not require interview techniques or special reference knowledge. Reference librarians, particularly in smaller settings, may spend a great deal of time helping patrons use the copy or microform machines, find a book in LC when they have been accustomed to the Dewey decimal system, or locate a particular issue of a periodical. Once the reference interview has been completed and a librarian has taught a patron to use appropriate tools, a courteous student assistant can then be invaluable in performing such tasks. Student assistants should also be used to run errands, retrieve materials from other parts of the building or system, or perform any other duty that saves time and legwork for librarians.

What has to be kept in mind is that stationing a student assistant at a reference area or desk is *not* providing reference service; hence the need to alert the library's patrons to the fact that a librarian is not on duty. Student assistants should clearly understand that they will be constantly referring patrons to paraprofessionals and professionals for assistance. They must realize that although they are extremely important to the public service work of the library, they can be of more help by making careful referrals than by trying to answer all patron queries, no matter what the level of difficulty.

Table 4-1. Reference Service Signs

Professional Reference Service
Is Available During
the Following Hours:

_____

_____

_____

At other times, our student
staff can offer limited
services

WELCOME

A Professional Reference Librarian
Is Now on Duty

WELCOME

A Professional Librarian
Is on Duty

Please Ask
the Student Assistant
to Refer You

SUGGESTIONS FOR TRAINING

Whatever the level of reference interviewing skills on the part of library paraprofessionals, it is a reasonably safe assumption that the level of skills in many libraries should be improved. Such improvement could begin with a staff member initiating a proposal and being allowed to carry the idea through. This approach is perhaps the most common and certainly reflects individual initiative, but it does not ensure either administrative support or coordination of efforts and results throughout the entire library. Staff initiatives may encounter lukewarm administrative support, which could actually scuttle or greatly reduce the possibilities of the initiative succeeding. Other scenarios, from hostility to benign neglect to enthusiastic support, will exist. However, the scenario that ensures success relies upon the philosophical and financial commitment of the library administration.

Librarians and library staffs do not work in a psychological or professional vacuum. As do all human beings, they respond to and are motivated by a reward structure. Such a reward structure may be altruistic and based upon sincere desires for professional development, or it may be based upon salary raises or job security motivations. More than likely, it is a combination of both. Nevertheless, some sort of reward structure exists in every organization, and both the professional and paraprofessional staff respond to it. The reward structure, be it recognition, opportunity for professional development, or financial gain, is to a large extent determined by the library administration. Thus, library administrators play a crucial role in the success or failure of any attempts to develop reference interviewing skills within the library staff.

The most visible way to show administrative support for continuing education is to provide opportunities for in-house skills development training. There are several ways this can be accomplished. The easiest program to initiate is a formal observation procedure whereby librarians discreetly observe paraprofessionals during the reference interview process and make suggestions for performance. Such observations should be conducted in an atmosphere of self-improvement rather than of evaluation of job performance. Although it is the easiest to initiate, there is a serious drawback to this method, in that reliance is placed heavily upon what one or two people think they observe rather than a documentary tape of what actually transpired. Nevertheless, for some libraries this may be a practical way to begin the process of evaluating reference services and helping to establish the concepts of the reference interview process.

Though more difficult to stage, videotaping of reference interviews may be the most effective method of improving reference interview techniques within a library environment. Actual situations and clients alleviate any concerns that the videotaping of reference interviews during training programs captures only an artificial situation conducted in a classroom setting. Obviously, the use of videotape equipment, unless hidden, will create some anxieties and questions among library patrons as well as librarians. A clearly displayed sign indicating that the reference desk is being videotaped for purposes of professional development should help the library patrons to understand why they are being taped, as well as publicizing the library's interest in continuing development. In other words, this should be perceived as a positive situation rather than a negative one. Nevertheless, it must be recognized that videotaping real situations has the potential to negatively affect both the quantity and quality of interviews, due to patron resistance or reluctance.

The method and depth of instruction would be less than that expected from the professional staff. Perhaps the most important benefit of videotaping paraprofessionals at the reference desk is the ability to teach the paraprofessionals when to stop searching and ask for the help of a professional librarian. If paraprofessionals are working unsupervised at the reference desk, the use of videotapes may be the only kind of feedback available to the professional staff to determine how successful, how useful, or how damaging the paraprofessional service at the reference desk actually is.

Videotaping entails the psychological drawback of having one's colleagues evaluate one's performance at the place where one works. An alternative approach is for the library administration to provide opportunities and funds for attendance at workshops, institutes, or formal training (as available). Such experience can be quite valuable, although the short duration of a workshop or seminar may not be sufficient to allow the long-term development of skills in the actual workplace. That is to say, when one attends a workshop or institute, reinforcement of skills may or may not occur on the job.

The same could be said of a third avenue for developing skills in reference interviewing—self-help. Paraprofessionals should be encouraged to read publications such as this book and articles on the reference interview process. Such a self-help approach naturally requires the initiative of librarians and administrators to undertake the project and then to maintain the motivation to develop and critique performance.

A fourth successful approach to introducing the subject of communication skills to staff members is through the use of commercial videos on the topic. Staff members can view the videotapes and critique the positive and negative factors presented. Pointing out the use of specific skills is enlightening to staff members who may be totally unaware that good communication requires hard work and specific skills. Because many tapes of this nature use humor or outrageous examples of poor interviews, sessions can be pleasant and fun as well as educational. Video- and audiotapes on the topic can sometimes be borrowed on interlibrary loan rather than purchased if cost is a factor. Some examples are:

Customer Service—More Than a Smile (Towson, MD: ALA Video/Library Video Network, 1991). Videocassette (13 min.).

If It Weren't for the Patron, directed by Jeff Lifton (Chicago: ALA Video, 1988). Videocassette (17 min.).

Kids Are Patrons Too! (Chicago: ALA Video, 1987). Videocassette (15 min.).

Maximizing Customer Satisfaction, featuring Arlene Farber Sirkin. (Towson, MD: ALA Video/Library Video Network, 1993). Audiocassette (45 min.).

Telephone Courtesy Pays Off (West Des Moines, IA: American Media, 1991). Videocassette (19 min.).

Paraprofessionals and student assistants are an important factor in the overall service attitude presented in the library. Consequently, it is important that their training include some awareness of necessary communication skills. In some cases training may have to be more concentrated. Planning and thought should be given to the overall service objectives of the library to determine exactly how support staff talent can be used to provide the best possible service.

NOTES

[1]Charles D. Patterson, "Personality, Knowledge, and the Reference Librarian," in *Reference Services and Technical Services*, ed. Gordon Stevenson and Sally Stevenson (New York: Haworth Press, 1984), 167.

[2]Nancy S. Osborne, "Librarian Humor in Classroom and Reference." ERIC Document #ED349018, 1992 (abstract).

[3]Ibid., 9.

[4]S. D. Neill, "The Reference Process and Certain Types of Memory: Semantic, Episodic, and Schematic," *RQ* 23 (summer 1984): 417–23.

[5]S. D. Neill, "Problem Solving and the Reference Process," *RQ* 14 (summer 1975): 314.

[6]Gillian Allen and Bryce Allen, "Service Orientation as a Selection Criterion for Public Service Librarians," *Journal of Library Administration* 16, no. 4 (1992): 68.

[7]Standards Committee, Reference and User Services Association (previously Reference and Adult Services Division), American Library Association, "A Commitment to Information Services: Developmental Guidelines," *RQ* 18 (spring 1979): 275–78.

[8]Egill A. Halldorsson and Marjorie E. Murfin, "The Performance of Professionals and Nonprofessionals in the Reference Interview," *College and Research Libraries* 38 (September 1977): 385–95.

[9]Marjorie E. Murfin and Charles A. Bunge. "Paraprofessionals at the Reference Desk," *Journal of Academic Librarianship* 14 (March 1988):12.

[10]Ibid.

[11]Julie Ann McDaniel and Judith K. Ohles, *Training Paraprofessionals for Reference Service* (NY: Neal-Schuman, 1993), 2–4.

[12]Kathleen Coleman and Elizabeth Magutti, "Training Nonprofessionals for Reference Service," *RQ* 16 (spring 1977): 217–19.

[13]"Standards for College Libraries, 1986," *College and Research Libraries News* 47 (March 1986): 197.

[14]Morrell D. Boone, Sandra G. Yee, and Rita Bullard, *Training Student Library Assistants* (Chicago: American Library Association, 1991), 69.

[15]Ibid.

[16]Nancy Emmick, "Nonprofessionals on Reference Desks in Academic Libraries," *Reference Librarian* 12 (spring/summer 1985): 158.

5

ON STAGE

There are many settings in which a reference interview can take place and a variety of situations in which verbal and nonverbal skills are essential for communication in libraries. The reference interview per se is not always conducted at a desk and may not even be conducted by a librarian in public services. Technical services librarians also have many opportunities to use interviewing skills. Among the many types of interviews with patrons that will occur, a few are

- Teaching interview
- Directional interview
- Information interview
- Bibliographic instruction interview
- Technical services interview
- Circulation interview
- Interlibrary loan interview

In each case, a professional librarian and a patron come together to try to understand the sort of information needed by the patron.

TEACHING INTERVIEW

The teaching interview has always been an important feature of academic settings and has become an increasingly important feature in public libraries as users interact more with technology. The teaching interview is the forerunner of more formal bibliographic instruction conducted for groups—often with a set curriculum. There are a number of ways to conduct the teaching interview. Using the 12 basic verbal and nonverbal skills, the librarian tries to learn the exact information need of a patron. The information need has a great deal to do with determining if there is a justification for teaching how to use a particular tool, or set of tools, or leaving the patron to do most of the searching alone.

A request that calls for a specific fact seldom requires a teaching interview. However, a request for help to gather materials for a bibliography may require some instruction. The librarian must also judge the patron's willingness to learn and motivation to keep searching after learning how to use a tool. If the librarian works alongside a patron, most patrons will be interested in helping to search through another periodical index, database, or other sources the librarian may recommend. However, there are always patrons who are perfectly content to have a librarian do all the searching. In many library situations, such as special libraries, it is automatically assumed that librarians will do all searching and, in fact, special libraries are generally committed to doing just that.

During a teaching interview, the librarian and patron finish the initial stages of the interview and actually use the library, its collections, and technology together. During a teaching interview, a librarian continues to pick up clues and use basic verbal and nonverbal skills. Keeping the following procedures in mind when conducting the teaching interview will help the process flow more smoothly.

1. Simplify. As the intermediary between the complex organization of the library and the patron, the librarian must simplify services, tools, and technology as much as possible. Do not burden the patron with detailed explanations of how a particular reference tool works, for example, unless a lengthy explanation is absolutely needed. Also, never ask the patron to learn about more sources than are necessary to answer the specific question at hand. In other words, a teaching interview is not intended to be all-inclusive library instruction, but instruction for the purpose of helping a patron meet specific information needs.

2. If you tell patrons that you (or some other librarian) will get back to them, be sure to do so. It is easy to get sidetracked in assisting other patrons, but politeness and the success of the interview demand that you follow up with the first clients.

3. Work alongside patrons for a while to make sure they understand what they have been told and how to use the resources (whether online or in other formats).

4. Do not try to teach a patron who refuses to be taught. Just because a school librarian, for example, believes that students should be taught how to use the library does not mean that every student feels the same way.

The teaching interview seems to be a natural and frequent happening in academic settings. In some institutions the teaching interview is sometimes formalized and called a *consultation*, a *term paper assistance program*, or *term paper counseling.*[1] In the more formalized programs, patrons generally make appointments with a reference librarian. A teaching interview, of course, can take place without an appointment.

The unique element of a teaching interview is that the librarian helps a patron find information by teaching how to use appropriate pieces of the library complex. Although it may take a bit longer to conduct, the teaching interview can be extremely worthwhile both to the librarian and to a motivated patron. Such a patron can use the knowledge gained again and again for similar information needs. Just as with any other successful reference interview, the teaching interview will give the patron confidence to ask again for help.

The teaching interview can present one possible problem. In certain settings, interview after interview may be devoted to teaching the same skills again and again. How often can a librarian explain entries in an index or a search in the online catalog before becoming bored? Most enthusiastic librarians do not get bored because the patrons change and the subject of the search changes. The variety of possibilities and combinations is endless and so, though one may teach the use of certain tools repeatedly, the context in which that teaching takes place varies. Variety of patrons and topics keeps the teaching interview interesting and productive.

DIRECTIONAL INTERVIEW

Directional interviews should be rather straightforward but can come in many varieties. The directional interview can be anything from a patron asking for directions to the restroom to finding out where something is located in another part of town. Simplification is the key. Keep directions simple and uncomplicated. Write them down for the patron when necessary. Two things are important to keep in mind. One is that a directional question is often the first one asked when a patron really needs information. The patron who asks "Where is the science section?" may really need information about building a bird feeder for the backyard. By answering, "Science books are located on the second floor. It's quite a large section. Can I help you locate something in particular?" and using nonverbal skills, the librarian will encourage the patron to provide more detail. The second thing to keep in mind is that many directional questions are just that. If a librarian tries an open question to ascertain if more information is needed, the librarian will often find that simple directions will do.

The fact that directional questions can mask more complicated information queries has caused librarians to debate the question of who should interview patrons. Should only librarians conduct interviews? Should paraprofessionals, clerical staff, and student assistants receive training to conduct interviews? The discussion of those and other questions is dealt with in chapter 4.

INFORMATION INTERVIEW

Information interviews occur when someone asks for information about the services of the library, for specific or nonspecific reasons. Information interviews generally develop in such a way that the librarian does more talking than the person making the inquiry. In fact, the librarian may be the one being interviewed. Information interviews are not to be taken lightly, because the times and circumstances in which they occur can be unsettling. The following examples illustrate the point:

- Several prominent alumni show up near closing time to take a look around and ask questions about services, staff, and so on.

- A local newspaper reporter stops at the reference area to ask how recent budget cuts are affecting daily operations.

- A student reporter wants to know if the library can provide good copy for the student newspaper.

- A librarian on vacation stops in to see how things are done, to get ideas, and to make comparisons.

- The vice-president of another division comes in to chat about the kinds of research services available to the people in the company.

These questions do not sound like the reference questions librarians struggle with in library school. Why even take the time to talk about such questions? Shouldn't they all be referred to the library director, supervisor, or someone else? For one thing, these situations occur more frequently than one might think and seldom seem to occur when all the appropriate authorities are around to deal with them. Furthermore, the information/reference desk is often the first service point in a library, the obvious place for questions to be asked. There is no right or wrong way to deal with such information questions. What is necessary is that all public service staff be aware that such situations will arise unexpectedly. Staff members should have an idea of policies, the extent of their responsibility, and some procedures for referral when necessary.

Librarians should be aware that information questions are not always straightforward. Other than awareness and discussion of such questions, it is also important to do some planning if possible. If a pattern seems to be developing, a reference librarian may want to have a few general responses prepared for reporters; create an attractive brochure or handout that describes the library's services; or review with public service staff the institution's or company's policies about the media. It may seem as though a simple request for information has been turned into a situation in which precautions must be taken and about which librarians should be nervous. Perhaps, but a patron's request for information, and the context in which that information will be used, can sometimes have financial, political, or other ramifications for the library and the parent organization.

These ramifications can be positive when handled well and with foresight. It is also perfectly acceptable to refer the questioners to a higher authority if that authority will actually be there.

BIBLIOGRAPHIC INSTRUCTION INTERVIEW

Reference librarians often are responsible for library instruction. *Library instruction,* as defined here, means instruction in the use of the library and its tools for a group, generally of students. Before such instruction can take place, the librarian should conduct at least one interview with the classroom teacher to determine what type and extent of instruction are necessary. The librarian must engage the instructor in a specific line of questioning and listen carefully. Although librarians should not give personal opinions or suggestions to a teacher, particularly in sensitive matters, they should feel free to offer professional advice on what types of library instruction are effective and to make suggestions for materials and use of time. When conducting the bibliographic instruction interview, the librarian must use a combination of closed and open questions to ascertain everything from the number of students to the methodology being used in the class.

Little attention has been paid in the literature to the interview for bibliographic instruction. Few instructors understand the nature of library instruction or exactly what it will accomplish and often assume that after one class session in the library, students will know everything about research. Actually, the library instruction interview may be a series of encounters with the instructor. First, the librarian or instructor may make initial contact to discuss the possibility of instruction. If the librarian is making the contact as a follow-up to student difficulties in the library, tact is certainly necessary. A positive offer of help rather than a suggestion of ineptitude in making assignments is always the best strategy. If initial contact is made by phone, tone of voice is by far the most important skill. In person, the other skills naturally come into play. If the teacher is receptive during the initial contact, the librarian should try to set up a specific appointment to talk about instruction.

During the second session, the most important interview takes place. Librarian and instructor work out goals and discuss possible methods and timetables. Generally this session requires privacy and an adequate amount of time. Open questions are essential. One might ask, for example:

- Can you give me examples of projects students will do?

- What do you want to accomplish in the class?

- What do you think library instruction can accomplish?

If the librarian is expected to produce teaching guides, worksheets, online sources, or other materials, subsequent meetings may be necessary to refine and edit these materials. After the initial contact, the encounters will become less formal, more on the lines of a conversation or meeting than an interview. Consequently, an important part of library instruction begins in the initial interview, where confidence and a working relationship are established. One should never underestimate the importance of the initial bibliographic instruction interview.

TECHNICAL SERVICES INTERVIEW

Technical services librarians who are just beginning in the profession are sometimes surprised by the number and extent of dealings they have with patrons. Helping patrons check on orders or interlibrary loans (if this is done by technical services staff), gathering statistical information for reports, identifying particularly complex citations, and making catalog or online interpretations are just a few technical services opportunities that require interviewing skills. Technical services staff should be included in discussions, workshops, and other meetings that might help them to develop and refine interviewing skills. In large libraries, librarians in periodicals, serials, or microform departments may staff a service desk to assist patrons.[2] Poorly conducted interviews in any part of a library can cause misunderstandings or lead to possible misinformation. All librarians should be alert to the public nature of their positions.

Beyond the attitude of individual librarians toward service, if there is a strong dichotomy or even tension between public and technical services staff, serving the patron becomes difficult. The administrative philosophy of the library has a great deal to do with the overall service given to patrons. If administrators are totally committed to providing the best possible service to users in every area of the library, that attitude will be transmitted throughout the library or system. Obviously, an administration openly committed to serving its clientele will facilitate and reinforce the public aspects of all librarians' dealings with users.

CIRCULATION INTERVIEW

An important service point where interviews are frequently conducted is at a circulation desk or counter. In the majority of libraries, the most obvious point of service is circulation, and patrons stop there first. In small libraries, all functions of circulation and reference may be combined into one service point. In most libraries, however, circulation may be the first place a patron asks for help. The circulation staff, then, needs to understand and use interviewing skills. The primary objective is to discern the nature of the patron's need so that he or she can be referred to another part of the library, or so that staff can handle the need right then. How successful the referral is often depends more on how the user phrases a question than on the interviewing skills of circulation staff. The user who asks for information about the concept of public policy has a good chance of being referred to the reference staff. In contrast, the patron who asks where the books about government are might very well be sent to the stacks in the appropriate classification, even though the real question was the public policy one. Except in specific directional questions, such as "Where is the copy machine?" circulation staff should be trained to ask at least one question of the patron just to aid the correct referral. In libraries where student assistants or pages are stationed at circulation, it is particularly important that they be aware that the first question is not always exactly what the patron wants.

INTERLIBRARY LOAN INTERVIEW

Several reasons exist for doing an interview for interlibrary loan. It is a chance to teach patrons how to use the service and the mechanics of it. It is also a chance to show a patron what is an acceptable bibliographic citation. The interview saves time, particularly if there are omissions and poor penmanship. Finally, the librarian has a chance to point out other resources the patron may have missed.

The interlibrary loan interview can be an extension of a reference interview, particularly if interlibrary loan and reference services are in the same unit. Wherever it is conducted, "[t]he skills used in conducting a good reference interview, both verbal and nonverbal, must be brought into play when guiding an interlibrary loan interview."[3] No matter what the setting, the interview with a patron requires the use of interviewing skills to discern precise information needs.

INTERVIEWING AND TECHNOLOGY

Mediated Searches

Technology has created new names for the people and activities that have been around for many years: end-users; client-searchers; online interviews; search interviews; presearch interviews; presearch counseling; and online ready-reference searching. Librarians are automatically the key intermediaries between patrons and technology, just as they are when dealing with traditional collections. The patron, end-user, or client needs the librarian to decipher, explain, and sometimes perform the fast-developing technological rituals of online database searching.

There are two common ways in which a user comes to the point of a presearch interview. Both involve a preliminary interview of some sort that usually takes place at the reference point. One approach is for the client to ask specifically for a computer search. In some cases, the user is confident of information needs, and the computer search is the answer. In other cases, the reference librarian must conduct an interview to determine if a computer search will be of any help to the patron. Taking into account the nature of the information need, time involved, expense, and so on, the librarian may be able to recommend that use of the library's traditional collection will yield the same or better results. In other words, not every patron who asks for online services understands all that is involved, including online limitations.

The second situation occurs when, in the course of the interview, it becomes apparent to the librarian that an online search would be the best way to meet the user's information needs. If the user agrees, the librarian, depending upon the organization, may do the presearch interview and search then and there. Otherwise, the patron may be referred to the online services department, asked to make an appointment at a later time, or use whatever other procedure is appropriate. One important point is that if the patron is present while an in-depth search is being done, it cannot take place at a public service desk. A librarian may be able to do a "quick and dirty" search at a reference desk, but it is best for all concerned to have some privacy for an online search.

Sara Knapp, in an article entitled "The Reference Interview in the Computer-Based Setting," makes some distinctions between the reference interview, which she sees as more personal, and an interview conducted as the prelude to an online search. "The reference interview in the computer-based setting is not radically different from the interview at the reference desk. The differences are generally more of degree than of kind. Problems and processes tend toward the cognitive side of the emotional-cognitive continuum." [4]

Sandra Lamprecht offers a viewpoint on how the search interview and the general reference interview differ. "A search interview does differ somewhat from the general reference situation in that the patron is more likely to know what topic he should like searched. He does not know, however, how to access the information needed for his topic utilizing the computer and, in many cases, he is also unfamiliar with the complexity and constraints of the 'searching universe.' " [5]

The interview during online searching must collect some specific information to form a successful search strategy. In formulating that strategy, the librarian must use appropriate verbal and nonverbal skills to elicit the full meaning of the patron's needs. The librarian probably uses more closed questions during the presearch interview simply because specific answers are needed.

Once the client and librarian are committed to an online search, it can become a delegated search or a search during which the user is present. A *delegated search* is one in which, after the interview is conducted, the librarian does the search without the user present. There are many articles discussing the relative merits of delegated versus user-present searches. In most cases, librarians tend to cut down on communication errors and improve overall search quality when the user is present. [6]

Generally, librarians doing online searching develop a set of prescribed questions to ask the patron, and those become the basis for most of the interview content. Even though a presearch interview tends to be more formalized, interviewing skills are still valuable. Initial eye contact, gestures, posture, facial expressions, and tone of voice will help to put the patron at ease. The two vital, verbal behaviors for the presearch interview are remembering and restating/paraphrasing content. Often an online searcher will write down what a patron is saying, which is an efficient way to conduct a successful interview. However, it works even better if one listens to the user, restates the content so that both parties are in agreement, and *then* writes down key words and phrases. By not writing things down immediately or going online the minute the interview starts, a librarian/searcher can save both time and money. The librarian's total, undivided attention to the patron at the beginning of the interview creates a positive professional image and allows for a more accurate statement of the information request.

Peggy Champlin, in "The Online Search," points out that online search patrons are usually given special attention with private consultations. She suggests that because regular reference patrons do not receive such special attention, this may be short-changing the traditional public.[7]

Helping Patrons to Use Technology

The instant and ever-changing popularity of CD-ROM databases, the Internet, and the World Wide Web has most librarians in a quandary as to the best methods and techniques for teaching patrons the use of online resources. A survey of librarians about teaching patrons to use CD-ROMs found that the preferred teaching method was one-to-one, point-of-use instruction. It also found that CD-ROMs have cut down on requests for mediated searches but cause busier reference desks.[8]

An interesting twist on the CD-ROM training that patrons want was found in a study by Gillian Allen. Allen discovered that overall, females rated training as more important than did males. Allen conjectured that "[t]his could mean that females are more insecure about using new equipment than males or that they are more willing to express a need for assistance. Females who do ask for help generally ask the librarian for help more than males, who tend to rely on their friends for assistance."[9]

A minimalist approach is expounded a number of times in the literature and its popularity appears to be gaining. The minimalist approach says that it is better to teach the novice less rather than more when teaching computer skills. Citing the work of IBM's John Carroll, Ralph Alberico states, "Minimalist design gambles on the expectation that if you give the learner *less* (less to read, less overhead, less to get tangled in), the learner will achieve more."[10]

Kristine Condic carries the approach further and applies it specifically to the one-on-one instruction that takes place between reference librarian and user. Her guidelines for the reference interview are:

1. Find out what the user wants.

2. Answer the question and only the question.

3. If the answer is too brief for the user to continue, the librarian should explain more to the user than was asked.

4. Be patient but brief with the user.

5. Indicate your willingness to assist users once they have tried things out on their own for a while.

6. If the user is still frustrated, make an appointment.[11]

The first guideline—finding out what the user wants—is the obvious place to begin the interview using verbal and nonverbal skills. Without knowing what the patron wants, which will determine if the CD-ROM and/or other sources are appropriate, the rest of the guidelines are moot.

Due to the expansion of CD-ROM databases, the interview becomes more interactive. The interview may expand from a single encounter to several as the patron works his or her way through various databases, along with other resources. The librarian moves away from the desk to join the patron at a workstation.[12]

In terms of online public access catalog (OPAC) and point-of-use instruction, the literature is sparse. It has been shown, however, that even when OPACs become more user-friendly, "users need and want human help even more than printed or online help."[13]

Throughout this chapter, the various settings and types of interviews in which librarians might engage have been discussed. The constant factor, no matter what type of interview, is the use of communication skills to ensure successful outcomes. Whether a librarian is designated primarily as a cataloger, circulation librarian, or reference librarian, there are ample opportunities to use interviewing skills to meet patron needs.

NOTES

[1]Kathleen Bergen and Barbara MacAdam, "One-on-One: Term Paper Assistance Programs," *RQ* 24 (spring 1985): 333–39; Tim Schobert, "Term Paper Counseling: Individualized Bibliographic Instruction," *RQ* 22 (winter 1982): 146–51.

[2]Helen M. Grochmal, "The Serials Department's Responsibilities for Reference," *RQ* 20 (summer 1981): 403–6.

[3]Virginia Boucher, "The Interlibrary Loan Interview," *Reference Librarian* 16 (winter 1986): 89.

[4]Sara D. Knapp, "The Reference Interview in the Computer-Based Setting," *RQ* 17 (summer 1978): 324.

[5]Sandra J. Lamprecht, "Online Searching and the Patron: Some Communication Challenges," *Reference Librarian* 16 (winter 1986): 177.

[6]Prudence W. Dalrymple, "Closing the Gap: The Role of the Librarian in Online Searching," *RQ* 24 (winter 1984): 177–83.

[7]Peggy Champlin, "The Online Search: Some Perils and Pitfalls," *RQ* 25 (winter 1985): 213–14.

[8]Cathy Seitz Whitaker, "Pile-up at the Reference Desk: Teaching Users to Use CD-ROMs," *Laserdisk Professional* 3 (March 1990): 32.

[9]Gillian Allen, "CD-ROM Training: What Do the Patrons Want?" *RQ* 30 (fall 1990): 93.

[10]Ralph Alberico, "Minimalist Approach to CD-ROM Instruction," *Lifeline* 44 (fall 1990): 1.

[11]Kristine Salomon Condic, "Reference Assistance for CD-ROM Users: A Little Goes a Long Way," *CD-ROM Professional* 5 (January 1992): 56–57.

[12]Domenica M. Barbuto and Elena E. Cevallos, "The Delivery of Reference Services in a CD-ROM LAN Environment: A Case Study," *RQ* 34 (fall 1994): 70.

[13]Jennifer Mendelsohn, "Human Help at OPAC Terminals Is User Friendly: A Preliminary Study," *RQ* 34 (winter 1994): 185.

6

BackdRops aNd PRops

THE REFERENCE MILIEU

It is all well and good to talk about specific interviewing skills and how they can be used during an interview. How luxurious it would be to be able to conduct interviews in an office with the door closed, to focus full attention on the patron. Obviously, librarians are not counselors and do not function professionally in the same appointment mode. In fact, librarians often function more in the mode of a retail business than the so-called helping professions. Therefore, in this chapter we discuss the general environment in which a public services interview is held, some of the constraints involved, and how the interview situation can change from library to library.

The Telephone

In any library, there are slow periods when a librarian has the luxury of taking time with a patron. However, many times the library is busy and patrons are waiting in line to ask questions while the telephone continues to ring. Somehow the telephone intrudes and seems to take total precedence over all other activities. In a library fortunate enough to have back-up staff, funds, and a willing administration, there are several solutions to the telephone at the public reference site. In a programmable phone system, incoming calls can be routed to another desk during peak reference times. Another possibility is "voice mail" or an inexpensive answering machine that will take names and numbers when the phone cannot be answered. A third possibility is to have a phone without an incoming line. Barring the possibility of any of those, a decision could be made not to have a telephone at a reference location.

If the reference department does have a telephone at the public desk and plans to do both telephone reference *and* personal reference service, then a telephone policy must be initiated and maintained. Such a policy should establish:

1. The priority telephone reference will receive.

2. How telephone reference will be handled when there are many in-house patrons.

3. Limits (if any) that will be placed on questions. For example, only three items will be looked up in the catalog, or no information will be given from the city directory.

Each reference department will determine its own needs. In some cases, a reference department may be so committed to answering calls that cordless, portable phones will be used.

The frustration level of trying to conduct competent, successful reference interviews while handling constant telephone calls and questions is *very* high. Librarians working in such an atmosphere must face the issue and make choices about service priorities that, if not totally agreeable, are at least feasible. It should also be remembered that the telephone conversation *is* an interview and that many of the skills used for in-person interviews apply.

Nonverbal skills, other than tone of voice, during a telephone reference interview are not apparent to the caller. "[N]egotiation is more difficult by telephone because the advantages of non-verbal communication are lacking."[1] An astute librarian may be able to discern additional information about the telephone patron through tone of voice, language capability, pitch of voice, or other clues.

A librarian's nonverbal behavior can be quite revealing to a patron who is watching the librarian handle a call. Even when the call is from a difficult patron, a librarian must be sure to convey a positive attitude so that patrons in the library do not detect a negative attitude. The nonverbal skill that will be noticeable on the phone—tone of voice—must be kept sincere and interested.

Remembering, asking open questions, restating content, and closing are the primary verbal skills to be used on the phone. Restating the contents of the question before hanging up is critical. It is vital to get pertinent facts and ideas during a call. Further discussion of telephone reference beyond the interview can be found in *A Librarian's Guide to Telephone Reference Service* by Rochelle Yates.[2]

The Appointment

It was stated earlier that librarians are not counselors and do not operate in an appointment mode. Normally, librarians have a certain amount of time designated for reference service when they are available for any patron. There are instances, however, when the patron would benefit greatly from making an appointment with a librarian and receiving full attention. Certain situations lend themselves to making appointments with patrons, and librarians should seriously consider setting up appointments. An academic environment lends itself well to appointments, whether with students, faculty, or staff. An appointment can be especially beneficial to a patron who is starting an extensive research project. In special libraries as well, there are many benefits to making appointments with clients. School and public libraries do not offer as many appointment possibilities, but often librarians assume that patrons want all help and information immediately when, in fact, they would be happy to set up a specific time to get undivided attention. Reference librarians, if they believe setting up an appointment would be helpful, should suggest it and try it. Not only are appointment interviews helpful to a patron, but they are also wonderful opportunities to practice interviewing skills and manage time better.

The view that librarians should make appointments is strongly expressed by Jitka Hurych in an article entitled "The Professional and the Client: The Reference Interview Revisited."[3] Hurych contends that only nonprofessionals should be used for public desk work and that professionals should handle all complex reference problems by appointment. Hurych also argues that librarians obtain more respect through appointments such as those that are the norm for online searching. In a different vein, Ruth Pagell presents a humorous situation in her article, "The Reference Interview," in which librarians see patrons *only* by appointment.[4]

It is highly unlikely that many libraries have the kind of trained staff it would take for librarians to work by appointment only. When considering whether to try any kind of preset appointments, the librarian should ask several questions.

1. Will the patron really benefit from a preset time, or is this just a delaying tactic?

2. Do I feel comfortable suggesting appointments to patrons?

3. Does the library have a clientele that often has complex requests?

4. If an appointment is arranged, is there an appropriate place to conduct the interview?

5. Do I have enough unscheduled time to try an appointment system?

6. Can I accept appointment cancellations and "no-shows" gracefully?

As well as considering the preceding points, the librarian should also think about the overall professional environment of the library and if appointments of any kind would fit the institutional setting. In a school library, where students and staff have limited time and access to the library, the librarian would find it difficult to make appointments. Some patrons in a special library setting might be willing to make an appointment, but in a high-pressure corporate situation it may not be acceptable. Only the librarian in the setting can determine the appropriateness of appointments.

In light of rapidly advancing technology, Jennifer Cargill predicts the need for appointment, consultative reference, particularly in academe. "The need for this service will intensify as need for detailed, specialist reference assistance or research guidance increases."[5] A staffing model emphasizing individualized research consultation by librarians is also espoused by Jackie Mardikian and Martin Kesselman. When librarians and paraprofessionals work together as a team, they provide a good situation for all concerned, particularly for patrons who get the most appropriate level of service for their needs.[6]

Philosophical Motivation

When discussing the general environment in which an interview takes place, it is important to consider the philosophical motivation behind the interview, in terms of supplying information versus teaching the patron how to use the library tools to find information. In an educational setting, the librarian has many opportunities to conduct both what might be called an information interview and a teaching interview. In the information interview, the librarian carefully determines the scope and details of the patron's information needs and then works to supply those needs. In special libraries, for example, after negotiating a question, a librarian works alone or with library staff to put together the information needed by the patron. In a school or college, the librarian often uses the request for information as a chance to teach the patrons how to use one or more tools to locate materials for themselves. Not all questions lend themselves to teaching interviews, and not all patrons want to be taught. The librarian who believes that all patrons should be taught to use a library and never be given information directly will certainly encounter resistance. In the case of complex information requests, trying to teach patrons how to go about the search would be tantamount to putting them through a formal reference course; hardly an efficient use of either the librarian's or the patrons' time. The teaching interview has even wider implications in libraries where end-users and technology come together.

Each librarian probably has a general idea of whether his or her philosophy is *always* to teach the patron to use tools or *always* to supply the patron's needs. Most library situations demand some of each, and it should be at the discretion of the reference librarian how best to handle each user. Problems occur, however, when a particular institutional or supervisor's philosophy is at odds with a flexible philosophy. A reference supervisor or library director may be strongly opposed to finding information directly for students; perhaps such a person feels that students are being spoon-fed rather than educated in library use. The reference librarian who feels compelled to teach each patron can be a frustration for a more flexible supervisor. Flexibility is the key.

Waiting Patrons

Another situation that will occur in any busy library is a line of patrons waiting to ask for reference help. Some wait patiently and some impatiently. In fact, some patrons will interrupt a reference interview if they feel their needs are more urgent or will just take a moment. All a librarian can do when facing a line of waiting patrons is try to remain calm and handle each request as it comes along. If possible, a librarian might be able to get a patron started on a search, but the places and tools in which the patron is searching must be relevant. One should never hand a patron a book just to keep him or her out of the way at busy times. If a librarian tells the patron that he or she will come back to help, he or she should do so. When helping several patrons, the librarian must use remembering skills not only within the confines of the interview, but also in getting back to patrons and recalling what they were working on.

One situation that occurs periodically is when a patron assumes that the librarian will remember a question asked a week earlier. Sometimes a librarian will, but because librarians see many patrons, it is understandable that they may forget the patron's earlier request. The librarian should consider such an event a compliment. Patrons who feel they have received good, personalized attention will assume that the librarian will remember. Actually, a successful librarian will need only to be reminded briefly to remember a patron's earlier request.

To summarize, a reference interview does not happen in isolation. Telephones may ring and there may be a line of waiting patrons. Librarians must face such problems by setting service priorities and policies. Philosophical questions about teaching patrons and supplying them with information must be addressed personally and institutionally. In all of the events that may transpire around and during a reference interview, librarians must continue to use flexibility in their approaches to patrons and situations.

Physical Setting

We take for granted that building a piece of furniture large enough to be formidable or high enough to nearly conceal the librarians when they are sitting behind it fends off potential users and develops the tendency to hide that lurks in many librarians. If you can't begin to meet your reference demands, this is the kind of desk to build, for it will drive away users in herds. Desks should [be] pleasant, unobtrusive, and placed so librarians can easily slide away from them quickly on either side. Their location speaks loudly of their importance or unimportance.[7]

Ellsworth and Joan Mason's wry comments are often closer to the truth than librarians would like to admit. Reference desks, counters, or service points can be formidable if designed more as barriers than as access points. For the general location of the reference service point, there are three critical requirements: visibility, proximity to entering traffic flow, and identification. Robert Pierson, in a landmark article entitled "Appropriate Settings for Reference Service," identifies 13 characteristics, along with these three critical ones, that every reference service area should have. They are:

1. Is readily accessible to incoming inquirers; service point is identifiable.

2. Is accessible to those who enter at points past the focal point.

3. Facilitates movement to other services and materials.

4. Facilitates one-to-one transactions.

5. Allows staff members to have a variety of interactions, e.g., extended conversations, group service, simultaneous one-to-one conversations.

6. Facilitates supervision of patron activity.

7. Can be used for staff paperwork, while remaining neat.

8. Facilitates access to reference materials.

9. Allows variation in the number of librarians and patrons present.

10. Has a flexible shape and layout compatible with technology.

11. Facilitates the work of other library units.

12. Promotes efficient use of personnel.

13. Resembles areas providing similar services.[8]

Although Pierson's characteristics apply to reference service in general, here we concentrate on the physical setup of the reference service point as it specifically relates to the interview. Obviously, the place to begin is with the service point itself. Should it be a desk or a counter, or does the reference librarian need a desk at all? A study of patron preference in types of service points showed rather dramatically that patrons almost universally prefer a counter to a desk when asking for service.[9]

"Counters have advantages which neatly balance the disadvantages of desks. They are more visible to approaching patrons, they are more easily identifiable as service points, and they facilitate interaction."[10] To consumers, travelers, and many other types of clients, the counter has become a symbol of service. Think about all the places where counters are the first stop in finding information: airports, banks, department stores, governments offices, hospitals, and on and on. Somehow the counter is more inviting. The most important factor is that at counter service points, eye contact is instantaneous and at the patron's level. When children are the primary clientele, a desk is probably preferable. However, some libraries have a set of stairs that children may climb to ask questions, to keep the counter height that appeals to adolescents and adults. This is particularly appropriate in libraries that have only one service point for all users.

Successful reference interviews can easily be conducted at a counter where eye contact is natural, as patron and librarian are at the same level. Counters are also extremely practical when the patron or librarian has something to show. For example, patrons often come to the service point with something written on a scrap of paper, a newspaper clipping, or even a rather heavy reference tool. The counter is an easy place for both parties to look at the exhibit, whatever it might be.

One of the disadvantages of a counter is that it does not provide an opportunity for the librarian to conduct certain types of extended interviews that require a considerable amount of time. There should be a table or desk close to the counter where patron and librarian can sit for an interview. This is especially helpful for elderly or disabled patrons. A group of patrons can be helped more effectively if all are sitting around a table with the librarian interviewing members of the group.

Library literature has recently recognized the need for two types of service points in one; that is, both a counter-height and a desk-height service point. When building a new library or redesigning the reference area, it behooves the staff to have both the counter *and* an adjacent desk-height counter. The desk-height counter is also valuable when working with patrons at a computer terminal. Joyce Crook, in an article about designing the perfect reference desk, talks about the decision to have a counter or desk. "The pace at the desk and the characteristics of the user should determine the height of the desk and whether or not to consider seating for patrons. In general, the greater the pace, the more [a] counter . . . , rather than a desk, should be considered."[11] At one large university, reference librarians at a desk found that if they did not immediately stand up when approached, students actually knelt down in front of the reference desk to get to eye level. This happened even though there was a chair next to the reference desk for patron use.

> Another consideration for design of service desks is the Americans with Disabilities Act architectural regulation that the service desk must have a portion of the counter that is at least thirty-six inches in length and that is no higher than thirty-six inches above the floor minus the thickness of the carpet.[12]

Setting up a two-level reference area is fine if new construction or remodeling is going on, or if the money is available to build such a service point. Many librarians, however, are stuck in archaic buildings that do not lend themselves to flexibility. Circulation and reference "desks" may be poured concrete. The service point may be tied by electrical, telephone, or computer installations to a particular configuration. For whatever reason, if the service point is the traditional desk, there are some possibilities to make it more approachable and conducive to an interview. The use of plants in strategic places can draw attention to the desk and also create an informal environment around the desk. At least one chair should be placed next to the reference desk so that a patron may sit. The best chair is one without arms, preferably straight-backed. Although this may not seem comfortable, getting in and out of a straight-backed chair is easier than any other. A lounge or easy chair may be difficult to get up from and may also be conducive to patrons settling in to chat. Some libraries place a low stool next to the reference desk, which could cause problems for elderly or disabled patrons. A reference librarian should be prepared to stand whenever a patron approaches the desk or remember to invite each patron to sit to get on the same level.

Another suggestion is to be sure that the reference desk is as free from clutter as possible. The sight of a librarian sitting at a desk that seems overloaded with papers and books will deter most users by indicating that he or she is too busy to assist them.

In most libraries, the most service-oriented spot is generally the circulation counter. Usually placed right inside the door of the library, its counter invites information queries. Most circulation counters are also quite long, with enough room for two or more staff members. Why not just call it the service desk? Reference librarians would be on duty right there where the major traffic flows. Actually, in many libraries there is no reason why the first person every patron asks for information should not be a librarian. It would thus be a librarian who makes referrals to circulation staff and any other service points. It would also be a librarian doing the question negotiation or reference interview immediately, without the patron having to make two stops. Certainly, in libraries with large circulations, this might not be practical, but in many situations it is. It is certainly worth a try in a building where a reference service point cannot, for whatever reason, be placed so that it meets the requirements of visibility, proximity to traffic flow, and identification.

Why have a desk at all? At various times, librarians have advocated doing away with reference desks per se.[13] The argument is that librarians should be circulating around the library when "on duty," helping patrons wherever they happen to be. In many cases, the librarian who always stands when the patron approaches, and moves freely away from the service point after or during the interview, does help the patron in many parts of the building. Reference interviews end up being conducted in the least expected places when a librarian has a reputation for being willing to help. One patron, watching another being helped, will proceed to ask for help too. The restroom, lunchroom, and various other places have sometimes been the settings for interviews that have continued later, sometimes into the library proper.

TECHNOLOGY AND SERVICE ENVIRONMENT

In the electronic library of today, the librarian's role—indeed, the whole staff's role—has expanded and changed. As the full range of services grows, actual answering of questions at a service point is only one of the many services reference librarians provide. "Taken at its most basic element, reference is an interactive process that is not tied to a physical place . . . in order for it to occur."[14]

The impact of electronic reference on the physical environment of libraries has been tremendous. Reference librarians find that additional space in an area adjacent to the reference service point is needed to supply more and more workstations for patrons, and find that they must roam or rove around the area to ensure that patrons understand the technology. Currently, there is no agreement on how reference should be set up in the electronic library. Many libraries cluster terminals; others spread them out. In recent books on library buildings, there are no formulas and few suggestions for deploying the hardware of technology. "Current reports indicate that library use increases in direct proportion to investments in automation."[15] Projections that library buildings will disappear or will soon be filled only with electronic devices seem to be on the wane. We are in a period of experimentation with the physical environment of reference and probably will be for the foreseeable future.

The main point to remember about the reference setting is that the interview process must be conducted successfully as a follow-up to the setting. In other words, a perfect reference service point that is visible and meets all the other requirements is a waste of planning if the professional is not interested in conducting the best possible interview and providing the best possible service.

Take a look at the reference service point in your library. Does it seem to meet many of the characteristics mentioned? Can successful interviews be conducted in the setting? Ask some patrons what they like or do not like about the service point. Ask other staff members. Consider changing the placement of the reference service point on a trial basis to see if it can be improved. Alternatively, consider having only one service point at what used to be called the circulation desk. Is a service point needed at all, or is service best provided without one?

The general atmosphere and physical settings in which reference interviews take place are important in several ways. Patrons must enter an atmosphere that is, above all, conducive to asking for and receiving appropriate service. They do not always understand why a particular atmosphere or setting is inviting, they just know it is and act accordingly. A well-planned environment creates an atmosphere that is pleasant to work in, with low frustration levels for librarians. By consciously working to eliminate telephone problems or poorly planned service points, related stresses can be reduced. Dealing pragmatically with the philosophical questions of service priorities and translating those questions into workable policies will add to the total professional environment. As a matter of course, librarians worry about the patron's needs, but they should also make sure that the general atmosphere and physical settings are comfortable and appropriate for the librarian as interviewer.

NOTES

[1]Rosemarie Riechel, "The Telephone Patron and the Reference Interview: The Public Library Experience," *Reference Librarian* 16 (winter 1986): 81–88.

[2]Rochelle Yates, *A Librarian's Guide to Telephone Reference Service* (Hamden, CT: Library Professional Publications/Shoe String Press, 1986).

[3]Jitka Hurych, "The Professional and the Client: The Reference Interview Revisited," *Reference Librarian* 5/6 (fall/winter 1982): 199–205.

[4]Ruth A. Pagell, "The Reference Interview," *Unabashed Librarian* 30 (1979): 8.

[5]Jennifer Cargill, "The Electronic Reference Desk: Reference Service in an Electronic World," *Library Administration and Management* 6 (spring 1992): 82–85.

[6]Jackie Mardikian and Martin Kesselman, "Beyond the Desk: Enhanced Reference Staffing for the Electronic Library," *RSR: Reference Services Review* 23 (1995): 21–28.

[7]Ellsworth Mason and Joan Mason, "The Whole Shebang: Comprehensive Evaluation of Reference Operations," in *Evaluation of Reference Services,* ed. Bill Katz and Ruth A. Fraley (New York: Haworth Press, 1984), 26.

[8]Robert Pierson, "Appropriate Settings for Reference Service," *Reference Services Review* 13 (fall 1985): 13–28.

[9]Linda Morgan, "Patron Preference in Reference Service Points," *RQ* 19 (summer 1980): 373–75.

[10]Pierson, "Appropriate Settings for Reference Service," 20.

[11]Joyce M. Crook, "Designing the Perfect Reference Desk," *Library Journal* 108 (May 1983): 971.

[12]Anne Wood Humphries, "Designing a Functional Reference Desk: Planning to Completion," *RQ* 33 (fall 1993): 37.

[13]Linnea Hendrickson, "Deskless Reference Services," *Catholic Library World* 60 (September 1983): 81–82.

[14]Lori Goetsch, "Reference Service Is More Than a Desk," *Journal of Academic Librarianship* 21 (January 1995): 15.

[15]Larry Dowler, "Our Edifice at the Precipice," *Library Journal* 121 (February 15, 1996): 118.

7

Rehearsals

So far we have discussed training for interviewing in terms of teaching the skill in the classroom. The techniques discussed concentrated on videotaping and audiotaping interviews for use in training. Such taping is time- and staff-intensive and can be somewhat disruptive to service if done with real patrons.

Training in interviewing skills can take many forms. As long as it is well planned, has content that is easy to understand, and helps staff to improve their individual skills, training will be a success. Professional trainers can be hired to teach interpersonal skills, but effective training can certainly be developed in-house. Interpersonal skills should be taught with methods and techniques that are interactive. Using a one-way presentation or lecture method is not conducive to interactive learning. The most appropriate ways to teach interviewing skills are through demonstration and/or performance, task exercises, and problem solving. "When you choose a method, remember that trainees are usually able to retain a great deal more of information when they are personally involved in the learning activity."[1]

IN-HOUSE TRAINING

To keep staff actively involved in training, there can be work exercises, case studies, and role playing. Structured discussion may also be useful for certain interviewing skills. It is neither necessary nor desirable to try to teach or learn all 12 verbal and nonverbal skills in one session. Working on only a few skills at a time is more appropriate.

Joanne Bessler's *Putting Service into Library Staff Training* provides a "Completed Sample Training Module" for telephone patrons. Using articles, a video, or case studies, the training module assists staff in dealing with patrons on the phone. Skills such as tone of voice, restating/paraphrasing content, and closing could certainly be incorporated into the module, which includes the following steps:

- Describe a patron type that staff may encounter on the phone.
- Help staff to think of the phone patron as part of the primary clientele.
- Have staff read related articles or watch an appropriate video.
- Develop case studies for discussion.[2]

Before talking about the case studies, specific interviewing behaviors could be discussed and practiced; that information would be useful for the case studies segment.

At all times during training, it must be kept in mind that adult learners have specific needs and wants that must be met. Adult learners, for example, want problem-centered learning. They are not as apt as younger students to accept theory or the word of an instructor at face value. They have a real need to relate what is learned to the problems and situations they encounter on the job.

The climate for adult learning must be interactive. Any trainer's manual is quick to point out that, unless the trainees are actively participating in training, the amount of learning that takes place will be fairly minimal.

Adults prefer to learn by doing, so practice in interviewing skills is needed before the skills become incorporated into personal style and habits. Whenever a skill is taught, there should be time to practice it.

Demonstration of skills is an important part of training. Through experience, the authors have found that staff want to see positive examples of skills being done well, although there is some benefit to seeing skills performed poorly. Demonstrations can be videos or role-playing using a preplanned script. If, as trainer, you simply do not have the time to create a reasonable demonstration, or you cannot find a video that fits the purpose, there are other interactive methods.

Work on task exercises can be done in groups or individually. The skills that lend themselves to exercises are asking open questions, using encouragers, and reflecting feelings verbally. It is an excellent idea for librarians and other staff to work on forming open questions with which they feel comfortable and would actually use in a real situation. Coming up with phrases and other ways to encourage a patron, and phrases to use to reflect feelings, also lend themselves to group exercises.

Case studies can be of great advantage by allowing staff to examine a situation that closely resembles a real problem or actual reference question. Staff can decide in specific detail how the interview might be conducted using open questions, encouragers, and so on. Case studies done in small groups will illustrate that the same situation or reference encounter can be handled successfully in a number of different ways.

An extremely effective way to develop relevant case studies is to put together a small group of staff to discuss their public service work and some of the problems (and delights) they encounter. Such a group can either give enough ideas to create some case studies or actually write the case studies. Case studies that come from real experience and situations are the most successful. No matter how well done case studies are in various books and manuals, some staff find it difficult to make the connection to their own work lives unless the case studies are set in a library.

Role-playing is one of the best ways for staff to practice interviewing skills. Role-playing can be done in front of a group but is also effective done in pairs, with partners. One partner begins by asking a vague reference query (this partner is the only one who knows what is really wanted). The other partner uses interviewing skills just as in an actual situation. After roles have been switched and played, the partners can critique each other in a relaxed and comfortable manner.

Descriptions and use of various training methods to reinforce any type of skill can be found in the many manuals and handbooks that deal with training and, especially, with training for customer service.

SELECTED RESOURCES FOR CUSTOMER SERVICE TRAINING MATERIALS

American Library Association Video/Video Library Network
320 York Road
Towson, MD 21204-5179
(800) 441-8373
http://www.bcpl.lib.md.us/~inlib/alavideo.html
Source for videos on customer service and reference in library settings. Video available entitled *Kids Are Patrons Too!* that deals with young people as library users in various situations.

American Media Inc.
4900 University Avenue
West Des Moines, IA 50266
(800) 262-2557
http://www.ammedia.com
Source for high quality videos, self-study books, and other media.

Crisp Publications
1200 Hamilton Court
Menlo Park, CA 94025-1425
(800) 442-7477
http://www.crisp-pub.com
Source for unique series of 50-minute books, as well as videos, computer-based training (CBT), and audiotapes.

CRM Films
2215 Faraday Avenue
Carlsbad, CA 92008-7295
(800) 421-0833
http://www.crmfilms.com
Source for high quality films and workbooks; provides a preview video catalog.

HRD Press
Human Resources Development
22 Amherst Road
Amherst, MA 01002-9709
(800) 822-2801
http://www.hrdpress.com
Source for ready-to-use workshop materials for customer service training, videos, books, and other training materials.

United Training Media
6633 W. Howard Street
P.O. Box 48718
Niles, IL 60714-0718
(800) 424-0364
Company represents many producers of training materials in video, CD-ROM, CBT, and self-study books.

Video Arts
8614 W. Catalpa Avenue
Chicago, IL 606056
(800) 553-0091
Company is a primary source for training videos produced by John Cleese.

NOTES

[1]J. Degado Figueroa, *Training for Non-Trainers: A Practical Guide* (Amherst: HRD Press, 1994), 42.

[2]Joanne M. Bessler, *Putting Service into Library Staff Training* (Chicago: American Library Association, 1994), 28–31.

8

ONE-PERSON SHOWS

LIBRARIANS WORKING ALONE

In all library settings, from special to school to public to academic, there are librarians who work alone, without the benefit of daily contact with other library professionals. These librarians have the same problems and encounters as any librarian dealing with patrons, but they also face some unique challenges.

As anyone who works with the public knows, dealing with other people all day long can be grueling, exhilarating, and exhausting. No matter what the setting, nature of patrons, or the librarian's skill, reference work is tiring. It also does not produce work output in the same way as cataloging, interlibrary loans, or circulation might. Even when a librarian is keeping track of the number of reference questions handled, the skill, time involved, and interview techniques employed never show up in statistics. In some specialized libraries that employ a single librarian, much of the reference work is through mail inquiries, and contact with patrons is so minimal that much time can be devoted to each patron. In other one-person settings, an enthusiastic librarian will probably develop programs, instruction, publicity, and the like to increase use of the facility and reference services. In such cases the librarian may create a situation in which one question follows right on the heels of another, with no breathing space between. Stamina, enthusiasm, and a sense of humor are very important here.

The need for breaks during extended work periods is also obvious but often overlooked. There are no statistics on how long one can continually work with patrons on reference questions before concentration and skills begin to wane. After years of experience, discussion of the problem with other librarians, and much observation, we believe that after three hours spirits can begin to flag. A high energy level, both

75

physical and mental, can be sustained for that length of time. (Of course, there will be disagreement with that figure, particularly as it is only a subjective opinion.)

Knowing such figures does not help the librarian who is literally on stage all day or all evening. Each librarian working with the public alone should study his or her own performance carefully for things that may affect it. Table 8-1 presents some questions a librarian should examine to better understand their energy patterns.

Table 8-1. Energy Pattern Checklist

1. During what times of the day do I seem to be at my peak?
2. During what times of the day do I seem tired?
3. Is there a particular time during the day when I begin to become irritable?
4. How often do I take breaks?
5. What do I do during my breaks?
6. Do I take a lunch or dinner break?
7. Do I make sure I get a change of scenery or environment during the day?
8. Do I understand exactly what the school, corporation, or institution expects of me in terms of public service? Are such expectations realistic? If not, why not?
9. Do I understand exactly what I expect from myself in terms of public service? Are such expectations realistic? If not, why not?
10. Do I understand exactly what patrons in this environment expect of me in terms of public service? If not, why not?
11. Do the answers to items 8, 9, and 10 match? If not, how can the three be reconciled?

Librarians, as with others in service professions, are constantly asked to give of their time, talent, and skills. Librarians must remember, particularly in the one-person setting, that constant giving can be a drain; professional life must and can be replenished in a number of ways. Obviously, attendance at local, state, and national library meetings, conferences, and workshops is important. Several librarians who are close geographically may want to meet informally once in a while to share experiences and lift each other's spirits. Reading the literature of the profession can help by generating new ideas or demonstrating that others are facing similar challenges.

Sue Bryant suggests several other ways solo librarians can keep up their motivation and intellectual acumen.[1] One way, particularly for special or school librarians, is to take advantage of in-house training offered by corporations, hospitals, or school districts. Such training may not be specially designed for librarians, but it can help the librarian develop a network and create other opportunities for learning. Offerings such as health and safety, technology, report writing, communication techniques, and so forth can be invaluable.

Staff exchanges within the same company, institution, or district enable the employer "to retain the services of an information worker who has specialized in the field and benefit from a fresh look at systems and services."[2]

Visits to other libraries can be an excellent means of staff development. Not only will it help in networking, but observation of others working with patrons can also bring new insights and ideas into play.

Writing and research, committee work, and involvement in professional activities are further ways the librarian working alone can augment the informal and serendipitous learning that happens daily.

When it comes to learning or improving specific interviewing skills, the task for the librarian working alone is more difficult. Reading articles and other materials about the interview and then trying to improve performance is the primary means of self-education. As good as a librarian's interviewing skills may be, there is always room for reinforcement, change, and improvement. Varying the use of techniques and concentrating on one skill at a time can be helpful. Table 8-2 provides some exercises the librarian working alone can work through at his or her own pace to improve skills.

Table 8-2. Self-Help Reference Interview Evaluation

Nonverbal Skills	**Verbal Skills**
Eye contact	Remembering
Gestures	Avoiding premature diagnoses
Posture	Reflecting feelings verbally
Facial expression/Tone	Restating or paraphrasing content
of voice	Using encouragers
	Closing
	Giving opinions or suggestions
	Asking open questions

1. Choose two skills from the list of interviewing skills. Read the brief description of each skill contained in chapter 2.

2. During each reference interview for two days, concentrate on the two skills you have chosen. Specifically work to incorporate those skills into your interactions with patrons.

3. After you have worked through all 12 skills, make two lists. One should be of skills that seem to work well for you and one for skills that are more difficult.

4. Study your two lists. For the next few days, work on only one difficult skill at a time during interviews.

Despite the difficulties and challenges of working alone, there are a great many positive things to be gained from being the only librarian in a library or a reference department. The librarian who works alone is the one who single-handedly sets the tone and environment in which service will take place. Getting to know the library's clientele well is another benefit of being the only librarian. By using well-developed interviewing techniques backed up by solid knowledge of appropriate tools and technology, one librarian can raise the esteem in which the profession is held. In each type of library, the librarian working alone can be a strong positive influence. A great deal of this influence depends on the librarian's ability to conduct dialogue in a relaxed and professional manner. Consequently, the use of interviewing skills is important in all dealings with people, not just in the reference setting. Table 8-3 lists types of libraries and the influences a librarian who works alone can have on such a library's clientele.

Table 8-3. How a Librarian Can Influence Clientele

Type of Library	Influences
Academic and School	♦ Act as a role model
	♦ Help to alleviate child and adolescent anxieties about libraries
	♦ Create an environment that students can enjoy
	♦ Create an environment in which faculty and administrators view librarians as colleagues
	♦ Contribute directly to the education of individual students
Public	♦ Alleviate public anxiety about asking questions
	♦ Create a positive image of librarianship
	♦ Contribute to individual patron growth
Special	♦ Contribute directly to the work of the organization through dissemination of information
	♦ Create a positive image of librarianship

In conclusion, being the only librarian can be a big advantage in terms of self-esteem, personal response from patrons, and the ability to create an environment in one's own personal style. The ability to interact with individuals is a critical part of such a position and the use of reference interviewing skills can only enhance that critical facet.

NOTES

[1]Sue Lacey Bryant, *Personal Professional Development and the Solo Librarian* (London: Library Association, 1995).

[2]Ibid., 40.

9

Special Performances

No matter what type of library situation a librarian is in, there will be times when a "special" patron will need assistance in using the library. Special users include children, teenagers, older adults, disabled patrons, international patrons, and angry or upset patrons.

DISABLED PATRONS

Public Law 101-363—the Americans with Disabilities Act of 1990 (ADA)—is "landmark legislation that extends civil rights protection to people with disabilities"[1] and is important as well as complex. In terms of reference service, the two areas of concern are Title II (Public Services), which includes service and accessibility. Services offered to disabled patrons must be equal to the services provided for all others. In other words, "[a] library may not furnish different services to library patrons with disabilities than are provided to others."[2] Because there are no specific rules to help libraries in the areas of service, a general rule is to provide all patrons with similar services.

Patrons' disabilities may range from small hearing losses to multiple speech and physical problems.

> Barriers to handicapped persons are primarily of two kinds—physical and attitudinal. Physical barriers include steps, narrow doorways, buildings without elevators, inaccessible toilets, and so forth. Attitudinal barriers include misconceptions about the capabilities of handicapped persons or feelings of being "uncomfortable" while trying to be of assistance. Such feelings are quickly communicated, discerned and often resented.[3]

81

Attitudinal barriers are those that can be eliminated during a reference interview. Every librarian has a set of prejudices, stereotypes, and attitudes that exist at any given moment, and such attitudes can extend to disabled persons. In library settings where there is little or no contact with disabled patrons, the appearance of one can produce stronger emotional response than if disabled patrons use the library on a regular basis.

In the past few years, the literature of librarianship has started to be more concerned with physically disabled patrons, and several articles and books have been written that give specific advice to librarians.

Hearing impediments are becoming more numerous as the general population grows older. There are two types of deafness. In a broad sense, *deaf* persons are those who cannot understand spoken messages by hearing alone. Those who are *hard of hearing* have some usable hearing and may be able to comprehend speech to some extent.[4] Deafness from birth is often accompanied by speech problems.

An important thing to remember when speaking to a hearing-impaired person is *always* to face the person directly. This will facilitate lipreading or allow the user to turn the better ear toward the librarian.[5] Speaking louder or speaking into a deaf person's ear seldom enhances the person's ability to understand. The profoundly deaf person will not hear, and speaking into a hearing aid, for example, may amplify sound painfully or distort it.

Facing the patron also allows the patron to see facial expressions. "The use of facial expression appropriate to the desired meaning and tone of the message is of considerable help in communicating with deaf people. . . . Facial expressions are also crucial in conveying the intensity of the message."[6]

If a librarian is having trouble getting a message across or cannot understand the patron after trying, writing is an excellent way to communicate. If an interpreter is present, talk directly to the patron, not the interpreter.

Warren Goldmann and James Mallory list eight tips on dealing with deaf patrons. The techniques are similar to what one would use with hearing patrons.

- Get the deaf person's attention before starting communication. Move into his or her line of sight or gently touch the person on the arm.

- Speak in a normal tone of voice. Shouting may embarrass the person.

- Enunciate without exaggeration.

- Use a moderate, uniform rate of speech.

- Paraphrase messages; try synonyms.

- Use appropriate gestures.

- Minimize head or body movements or other behaviors (gum chewing, for instance) that would make lipreading more difficult.

- Remember that writing can be very effective.[7]

Visual impairments can be accommodated in several ways, depending upon the extent of blindness. Seating in good light, where noise levels are not distracting, can help.[8] The librarian may need to use touch, explain what he or she is doing, and tell what obstacles are in the way. The patron may have a reader or companion. The librarian should deal directly with the patron who has the question rather than the companion, who may have little idea of the patron's information need.

If the blind person has a guide dog, never pet or feed it. When asked for directions, a librarian should use explicit terms and avoid terms such as "over there" or "turn this way." When helping a blind person to sit, place a hand on the side or back of the chair.[9]

Mobility or neurological difficulties may require the patron to use a cane, crutch, walker, wheelchair, or other device.

> The librarian should be observant of the capabilities of disabled patrons to avoid such situations as handing a book to a patron who has limited arm movement or manual dexterity. If the librarian can think of offers of assistance to disabled patrons as being similar to offering to open a door for someone with both arms full of books, the offers of help will not be a favor but a way of being polite, as they should be.[10]

For a patron in a wheelchair, there are a few basic, commonsense rules. Sitting down to be at eye level is effective and helps put the patron at ease. It also helps the librarian to see facial expression and to hear the patron more clearly. Situate yourself directly in front of the disabled person. "Wheelchairs, crutches, or other appliances used to enhance physical abilities are very personal items. They should not be borrowed or handled without permission. In particular, they should not be moved from the reach of the owner."[11] Table 9-1 on page 84 provides other ideas for working with disabled patrons.

Even if librarians seldom deal with permanently disabled patrons, there are those who are *temporarily disabled*. The patron with a broken or sprained limb, recovering from serious surgery, experiencing severe back pain, or suffering from some other ailment is as disabled for the duration of the impairment as the permanently impaired patron. In fact, the temporarily disabled patron may have a lower frustration level and actually be more difficult during a reference interview. No matter what the disability, the librarian should avoid premature diagnosis or assumptions about the patron's problems or status, just as with any library user.

Table 9-1. Working with Disabled Patrons

No matter what kind of disability or impairment a patron has, there are some general, basic rules that the experts agree are useful to the communication between librarian and disabled patrons:

◆ Focus on the person, *not* the disability. Asking personal questions about a disability is inappropriate.

◆ Speak directly to the disabled person, no matter who else is accompanying him or her.

◆ Do not be embarrassed to use words or phrases such as "you can see for yourself" to a blind person or "let's walk over to the atlas table" to a person in a wheelchair. Disabled people use such phrases themselves.

◆ Empathy, not pity or sympathy, is the appropriate emotion.

◆ Use written communication if necessary.

◆ Remember that disabled patrons can be moody, rude, or ill-mannered. Not all communication failures are the fault of the librarian.[12]

YOUNG PATRONS

Children and teenagers make up a sizable percentage of the users of public libraries. Much is written about work with young patrons in terms of actual reference tools, uses of specific types of children's books, and other materials-oriented subjects. Literature about the reference transaction with children, though, is limited. A body of work exists in education, particularly aimed at studying how teachers ask or should ask questions. Works by authors such as Deborah Cassidy[13] and Mark Allerton,[14] for example, concentrate on determining what types of questions solicit specific cognitive demands of children. That is, there are low-level questions that "demand recall of facts, comprehension and explication, while higher-level questions demand analysis, synthesis, and evaluation."[15]

Recent years have also seen a growing body of literature, in psychology and law, about the questioning of children who have been victimized or who have observed criminal acts. Though dealing with an unfortunate and unpleasant context, some of this work does point out ways to avoid asking leading questions, that is, questions to which the child wants to give an answer the adult expects.

Determining a patron's actual information need is the critical factor in reference work. "[I]t can be particularly problematic when dealing with children who form their questions through limited vocabulary and sphere of experience."[16]

Linda Callaghan identifies special considerations that should be taken into account when conducting reference interviews with children. Most important are finding the "real" subject area, figuring out how much information is needed, determining the most useful form of information, and finding the appropriate reading level.[17]

There are a number of interesting and important differences between reference interviews with adults and those with young patrons. More so than adults, children may hesitate and be intimidated about approaching an adult for help. Kathleen Horning suggests that "[a]dult reference puts most of its attention on what appears after the question is asked. Children's reference puts more attention on what happens before the question is asked because children are simply not as skilled at asking questions."[18]

Another difference between reference for adults and reference for young users is that the interviewer can take nothing for granted with children in terms of vocabulary, understanding of how a library works, or prior knowledge about a subject. It is particularly easy, with young users, to diagnose all questions prematurely as dealing with a school assignment. Children's curiosity goes beyond the bounds of school or daycare and will extend to their other activities, such as Scouts or 4-H—as well as simply a genuine information need for a personal interest.[19] Children have more limited vocabularies than adults. Asking children if they want fiction or nonfiction can be problematic, but asking "Do you want a story with a truck in it, or do you want a book that will tell you all about different kinds of trucks?" should be more successful in discovering the "real" need.[20]

Age is another factor to be considered. Kathleen Horning gives excellent descriptions and examples of the way children ask questions, from the two-year-old who succinctly asked, "What you got?" to the 11-year-old who asked for "geographic books" (he really wanted a book about whales) because he thought that was how an adult would phrase it.[21]

Table 9-2 on page 86 contains five imaginative interviewing tips from Melody Allen[22] for working with young children under the age of eight.

The three-party interview is characteristic of work with young people. The three-party interview "can be complicated, frustrating and sometimes downright awkward."[23] Three-party interviews have various configurations, such as

- Child and parent
- Child and teacher (the teacher may not be present physically, but is part of the interview nonetheless)
- Teenager and friend(s)

Charlene Strickland, in an article called "Young Users," categorizes the child and parent three-party interview even more. In the "open-minded child and fearful parent" encounter, the parent may be fearful of using the library at all, or perhaps has no acquaintance with the new technology. As the librarian helps the child, it is important not to embarrass the parent. Translating jargon into user-friendly explanations and never talking down to either parent or child is crucial.

Table 9-2. Working with Young Children

1. Don't start by talking or asking questions. Start with the child's agenda, and you'll get more cooperation and openness with your own.

2. Let the child hold a puppet, doll, stuffed animal, or toy. If you ask the object your questions, the child in this age group will generally give his/her own answer.

3. Underreact rather than overreact. Keep the focus on the child's statement, not on your reaction. Avoid praise, as the child will be wary that the next time may elicit criticism instead of praise.

4. Allow the child to use nonverbal responses and to use his/her whole body. Ask "show me."

5. Give the child enough time for his/her agenda as well as for your own.

Source: Melody Lloyd Allen, "Talking with Young Children in the Library," *American Libraries* (October 1989).

In the "silent child and know-it-all parent" threesome, the goal is to speak with the child without alienating the parent. Always focus on the child and confirm that the need expressed by the parent is really what the child needs or what the teacher suggested. Being at eye level with the child is particularly useful in this situation. It makes a nonverbal statement that the child's needs are important.

Finally, the "parent unaccompanied by the child" is a difficult interview because the parent may not have all the pertinent information. While one does one's best to help, one can always suggest that it is always helpful to have the child present.[24]

Teens are likely to be at a library with friends. Even when there is a one-to-one conversation with a teenager, there is often a "giggling friend or peer group that's too cool to ask for help, so that often in dealing with teenagers there is this very strong sense of third-party presence."[25]

There is no way to completely avoid the three-party interview. In many cases, the third person, especially a parent, can actually be very helpful in soliciting information from the child; clarifying a child's choice of words; or, merely by being present, giving the child a nonthreatening environment in which to ask questions.

In reference interviews with young users, the same verbal and nonverbal behaviors should be used as with adults. Children and teens should be treated with respect. "Careful attention to verbal communication and body language can improve the child's perception of the helpfulness of staff. By keeping conversational tone low and moving away from crowds, the library staff conveys respect for the privacy of the child's questions and the child's right to ask questions on any subject."[26] Table 9-3 lists tips for works with children and teens.

Table 9-3. Working with Children and Teens

- ♦ Ask open-ended questions as much as possible.
- ♦ Paraphrase and restate the question.
- ♦ Simplify library jargon.
- ♦ Find out limitations on format or reading level.
- ♦ Do not presume that each question stems from schoolwork.
- ♦ Respect the young patron's individuality and privacy.
- ♦ Focus attention on the young user in a third-party interview.

Among teenagers, stuttering is the most common speech disorder.[27] There are some important guidelines for speaking with a stutterer. First, do not call attention to the problem; it will probably make the teenager tense and can lead to more stuttering. Secondly, do not ask the stutterer to relax or speak more slowly.[28] Third, do not try to anticipate what the stutterer is saying or try to finish sentences.[29]

OLDER ADULTS

In 1990, there were 53 million Americans over the age of 55 and 31.6 million over age 65. Obviously, with that many older adults, some will use libraries. The "Guidelines for Library Service to Older Adults," prepared by the Library Services to an Aging Population Committee of the Reference and User Services Association of ALA, suggest ways in which to meet the needs of older adults.

For the one-on-one interaction between a librarian and an older adult, the guidelines state that librarians should "[e]xhibit and promote a positive attitude toward the aging process and the older adult."[30] In an article interpreting the guidelines, Celia Hales-Mabry notes that many people have ambivalent attitudes about getting older.[31] If a librarian is uncomfortable with the aging process, the attitude may exhibit itself in impatience or an assumption that additional help or louder speech is always needed.

Important factors in conducting interviews with older adults are the basic characteristics of adult learners, as shown by research. "Adults prefer to control the pace of learning activities, to learn independently, to use discussion to reinforce and stimulate ideas, and generally to take a more active and controlling part in the learning activities in which they are engaged."[32] Added to these adult learning factors is the fact that older, retired adults have more time to slow down and enjoy encounters with other people and may feel less inclined to hurry for others. Thus, librarians must be alert to a subtle shift in the way the interview is conducted. Connie Van Fleet cites three specific ways in which reference transactions may serve the older adult more effectively.

- **Patience**. Because older adults feel less inclined to hurry and like to take time to understand tasks before starting, a positive and patient attitude is needed to match the pace set by the patron.

- **Sensitivity to unspoken needs**. No special treatment is needed for most older adults; however, some are hesitant to ask for help, feeling they are troublesome to the librarian. Using phrases such as "May I do anything for you?" or "Please don't hesitate to ask if you need anything else" will reassure such persons.

- **Flexibility**. Vision and hearing are sometimes diminished with age. Some older adults may need accommodation.[33]

Van Fleet goes on to offer specific suggestions for useful techniques during the interview.

It is rather natural to repeat a comment if a patron leans forward, places a hand behind the ear, looks puzzled, or asks what was said. Looking directly at the patron, speaking in a measured and clear, but not exaggerated, voice and keeping hands, gum, and hair away from the mouth will also enhance interaction. Keeping a pad and pencil handy for writing notes will help clarify information for all patrons, not just those who have difficulty in hearing.[34]

Combining extra sensitivity, flexibility, and patience with the usual verbal and nonverbal behaviors of good reference interviewing will help a librarian to be successful in meeting the needs of older adults.

INTERNATIONAL PATRONS

Librarians sometimes serve immigrant and student populations with unique language, cultural, and social structures. The librarian who can speak to those patrons in their native tongue is indeed fortunate. Most Americans, however, do not speak a second language, so, in a way, both patron and librarian are disabled. To standardize the terminology, we use the term *international patron* for those who are students studying in the United States and for all others for whom English is a second language.

It is estimated that approximately 408,000 international students use libraries in colleges or universities every year.[35] On some campuses only half a dozen international students are enrolled, whereas on others they may number in the hundreds. Other than language, international patrons also exhibit cultural differences,

differences in learning styles and behavior, different body language, and knowledge of libraries that may not parallel that of the American patron.

When dealing with an international patron, interviewing skills must be examined to determine how each might be used to best advantage. Nonverbal behaviors—eye contact, gestures, body posture, and tone of voice—vary from culture to culture. Time and space concepts also vary in different cultures. People from the Middle East, for example, may stand very close in normal conversation, a stance that may cause discomfort to an American, particularly a woman. American women are viewed in many cultures as open and frank. However, it is not unusual for a male student from certain cultures to make advances to a woman who looks him straight in the eye, smiles, leans toward him, or gives him individual attention, when all she intended to do was to use her best professional manner to determine his information needs.

The same verbal skills, obviously, should be used with all patrons, but the international patron presents some special challenges. A thick accent or poor command of English, or a combination of both, can create real communication problems. One thing that seems to happen often is for a patron, when asked if he or she understands, to say yes so as not to admit that there is little comprehension. Look for other cues to confirm understanding. Ask patrons politely to repeat what has been said or go with them to make sure they do understand. If the librarian doesn't understand patrons, he or she should ask them to repeat what they said or to write it down. Perhaps someone else on the staff is better at understanding accents, or even speaks the language. Librarians may even use other patrons to help in the communication process. Some other general ways to improve communication are: "Avoid using complex sentence structure and vocabulary. Avoid using library jargon unless absolutely necessary. Avoid using slang, allusion, metaphor, jokes, and unfamiliar references."[36]

If a library serves one or more populations that speak a particular language and use the library often, it might be advantageous for librarians to learn some helpful phrases and perhaps know some library terms in that language. A helpful guide to look at is Patricia Promis and Maria Hoopes's ¿Habla Español? No, But I Can Try to Help You. It includes some phrases and words to help with directional questions, the reference interview, and a glossary.[37]

Laughter is universal, and humor is often thought to be just as international and universal. "Humor differs widely from culture to culture. Consequently, it should not be attempted except at the most basic level, and even then with caution and with an awareness that, if a joke falls flat, one should move quickly on and not compound the problem by attempting explanations."[38]

Encouragers are important in speaking with international patrons. Positive body language and short phrases such as "tell me more" or "keep talking, I'm listening," said with a smile, will help the user to relax and tell more about what is needed.

Status may also be a problem in dealing with international patrons. Students, for example, may come from the wealthy and upper classes of their own countries, and "librarians may be regarded as nothing more than clerks."[39] Nothing offends

American sensibilities more than being treated condescendingly, but an awareness of the unintentional cause can alleviate the situation.

The educational and library backgrounds of international patrons vary greatly. For example, "[i]n many developing countries, the educational systems tend to be more rigid, with a greater emphasis on rote memorization and recitation than on the development and application of original ideas."[40] Consequently, students may not enter into open discussion or question what the instructor, textbook, or librarian says, even when they do not understand.

Immigrant populations throughout the United States bring with them an ignorance of American library systems and, in many cases, awe of professionals and the availability of so many "free" books and other materials. Tamiye Trejo and Mary Kaye, in an article about immigrants, point out differences among cultures and the libraries of other countries. They also note that librarians should be aware of the timidity, awe, and fear of public institutions that many immigrants bring with them.[41]

ANGRY OR FRUSTRATED PATRONS

A burgeoning amount of literature deals with troubled and troublesome patrons in libraries. Violence, unattended children, the homeless, the mentally ill, sexual deviancy, and vandalism show up on television screens, in newspapers and magazines, and in libraries. The purpose of this discussion is not to delineate all the correct behaviors staff members should exhibit for each type of patron, though we have listed some sources at the end of this chapter for those who want more information. Here we concentrate on the reference interview and dealing with upset or frustrated patrons, particularly those who are angry or frustrated by the library or their information need.

Although the verbal and nonverbal skills for such interviews remain the same as for other interviews, additional skills are often helpful. In a chapter on angry people, in her book *It Comes with the Territory*, Anne Turner offers several useful skills:

- Active listening
- Paraphrasing
- "I believe you"
- Stand and deliver[42]

In active listening, the librarian acknowledges the patron's feelings. ("It sounds as though you're angry about this policy.") That helps the patron sense that the librarian cares and helps to diffuse some of the anger. By paraphrasing what the patron is saying, the interviewer makes sure what the "real" problem is. The patron who hears the words, "I believe you," begins to feel that he or she is trusted and tends to calm down. The stand-and-deliver technique is a difficult one for staff, because it means that "the staff person stands there and the patron delivers anger."[43] Eventually the patron winds down and the staff can start reasonably to solve the problem. This technique is only useful when a patron is furious and needs to vent.

"Avoidable Upsets" is a term used by Rebecca Morgan in her book *Calming Upset Customers*. These upsets are ones that your organization has some responsibility for causing. Examples include:

- Someone promised something that was not delivered.
- A staff member was indifferent, rude, or discourteous.
- A staff member has an unpleasant attitude.
- The patron does not feel that he or she was listened to.
- The patron was given a smart or flip reply.
- The patron's honesty or integrity was questioned.
- A patron is embarrassed at doing something incorrectly.
- A staff member argued with the patron.[44]

Whether a patron is upset by something the library staff did or did not do or by something for which the library is not responsible, the staff's choice of words and phrasing is important to showing a helpful, positive attitude. The three primary rules are: avoid giving orders, take responsibility, and avoid causing defensiveness. Do not say "You have to." Give the patrons options or ask them pleasantly to do something and explain how it will help the situation. Tell the patron what you *can* do, not what you cannot or will not do. Do not criticize patrons for doing or saying something wrong. Work together with them, as well as other staff members, to rectify the situation. "Learning to calm upset people is not easy. There is no single technique that works with every upset person. But there are skills that can be learned, with a positive attitude and practice."[45]

Although the skills needed to interview the special patron are the same as those for any other patron, certain intangible qualities will be of use. More patience and persistence may be needed to work with special patrons. Most important to the success of such interviews are a sense of empathy, acceptance, and belief in the intrinsic value of the individual, no matter what the disability. Disabled or international patrons should not be viewed as problems, but rather as seekers of information who have unique qualities.

Additional Resources for Dealing with Troubled, Disruptive, Angry Patrons

The End of the Line (Des Moines, IA: American Media, 1992). 1 videocassette (15 min.); 1 training leader's guide.

James L. Groark, "Assertion: A Technique for Handling Troublesome Library Patrons," *Catholic Library World* 51 (November 1979): 172–75.

Joseph J. Mika and Bruce A. Shuman, "Legal Issues Affecting Libraries and Librarians: Employment Law, Liability and Insurance Contracts and Problem Patrons," *American Libraries* 19 (April 1988): 314–17.

Rhea Joyce Rubin, "Anger in the Library: Defusing Angry Patrons at the Reference Desk (and Elsewhere)," *Reference Librarian*, no. 31 (1990).

Charles A. Salter and Jeffrey L. Salter, *On the Front Lines: Coping with the Library's Problem Patrons* (Englewood, CO: Libraries Unlimited, 1988).

N. M. Smith and I. Adams, "Using Active Listening to Deal with Problem Patrons," *Public Libraries* 30 (July/August 1991): 236–39.

Evan St. Lifer, "How Safe Are Our Libraries?" *Library Journal* 119 (August 1994): 35–39.

NOTES

[1]Nancy C. Pack and Donald D. Foos, "Library Compliance with the Americans with Disabilities Act," *RQ* 32 (winter 1992): 255.

[2]Ibid., 259.

[3]William L. Needham, "Academic Library Service to Handicapped Students," *Journal of Academic Librarianship* 3 (November 1977): 274.

[4]Warren R. Goldmann and James R. Mallory, "Overcoming Communication Barriers," *Library Trends* 40 (summer 1992): 22.

[5]Gilda Berger, *Speech and Language Disorders* (New York: Franklin Watts, 1981), 41.

[6]Goldmann and Mallory, "Overcoming Communication Barriers," 24–25.

[7]Ibid., 28–29.

[8]Ibid.

[9]"When You Meet a Disabled Person" (Seattle: University of Washington, Disabled Student Services, November 1988) (brochure).

[10]Francesca Allegri, "On the Other Side of the Reference Desk: The Patron with a Physical Disability," *Medical Reference Services Quarterly* 3 (fall 1984): 69.

[11]Chalda Maloff and Susan M. Wood, *Business and Social Etiquette with Disabled People* (Springfield, IL: Charles C. Thomas, 1988), 22.

[12]Ibid., 68–69; Ruth A. Velleman, *Serving Physically Disabled People: An Information Handbook for All Libraries* (New York: R. R. Bowker, 1979), 19–20.

[13]Deborah J. Cassidy, "Questioning the Young Child: Process and Function," *Childhood Education* 65 (spring 1989): 146–49.

[14]Mark Allerton, "Am I Asking the Right Questions? (What Teachers Ask of Children)," *International Journal of Early Childhood* 25, no. 1 (1992): 42–48.

[15]Cassidy, "Questioning the Young Child," 146.

[16]Linda Ward Callaghan, "Children's Questions: Reference Interviews with the Young," *Reference Librarian* 7/8 (spring/summer 1983): 55.

[17]Ibid., 58–59.

[18]Kathleen T. Horning, "How Can I Help You? The Joys and Challenges of Reference Work with Children," *Show-Me-Libraries* 45 (spring/summer 1994): 9–19.

[19]Callaghan, "Children's Questions," 56.

[20]Horning, "How Can I Help You?" 15.

[21]Ibid., 18.

[22]Melody Lloyd Allen, "Talking with Young Children in the Library," *American Libraries* (October 1989): 926–28.

[23]Horning, "How Can I Help You?" 18.

[24]Charlene Strickland, "Young Users," *Wilson Library Bulletin* 63 (May 1989): 96–97.

[25]Horning, "How Can I Help You?" 14.

[26]Vicky L. Crosson, "Hey! Kids Are Patrons, Too!" *Texas Libraries* 52 (summer 1991): 49.

[27]Berger, *Speech and Language Disorders*, 41.

[28]Ibid., 48.

[30]Reference and Adult Services Division, American Library Association, "Guidelines for Library Service to Older Adults," *RQ* 26 (summer 1987): 444.

[31]Celia Hales-Mabry, "Serving the Older Adult," *Reference Librarian*, no. 31 (1991): 70.

[32]Connie Van Fleet, "A Matter of Focus: Reference Services for Older Adults," *Reference Librarian*, no. 49/50 (1995): 150.

[33]Ibid., 152.

[34]Ibid.

[35]Suzanne Irving, "Addressing the Special Needs of International Students in Interlibrary Loans: Some Considerations," *Reference Librarian*, no. 45/46 (1994): 111.

[36]Louise Greenfield, Susan Johnston, and Karen Williams, "Educating the World: Training Library Staff to Communicate Effectively with International Students," *Journal of Academic Librarianship* 12 (September 1986): 230.

[37]Patricia Promis and Maria Segura Hoopes, *¿Habla Español? No, But I Can Try to Help You: Practical Spanish for the Reference Desk* (Chicago: RASD/American Library Association, 1991).

[38]Gina Macdonald and Elizabeth Sarkodie-Mensah, "ESL Students and American Libraries," *College and Research Libraries* 49 (September 1988): 429.

[39]Sally G. Wayman, "The International Student in the Academic Library," *Journal of Academic Librarianship* 9 (January 1984): 339.

[40]Greenfield, Johnston, and Williams, "Educating the World," 229.

[41]Tamiye Fujibayashi Trejo and Mary Kaye, "The Library as a Port of Entry," *American Libraries* 19 (November 1988): 890–92.

[42]Anne M. Turner, *It Comes with the Territory: Handling Problem Situations in Libraries* (Jefferson, NC: McFarland, 1993), 46–50.

[43]Ibid., 50.

[44]Rebecca L. Morgan, *Calming Upset Customers: Staying Effective During Unpleasant Situations* (Menlo Park, CA: Crisp Publications, 1989), 14–15.

[45]Ibid., 2.

10

The Critics and Reviews

WHY EVALUATE?

Every book on management, personnel, and library service emphasizes the need for evaluation of the activities of whatever institution or organization is being managed. *Evaluation* can mean anything from counting whatever is countable and comparing it to a previous year, to generating comprehensive stacks of forms and surveys to document what is taking place and how well people are performing. The truth of the matter is that many organizations do no evaluation at all, and become concerned about it only when there is an unsatisfactory employee and no written documentation of poor performance. It is easy to count the number of items cataloged and, particularly with the onset of online technical services, to set goals for each cataloger in terms of the amount of time spent on each item, and so on. Some other services, particularly circulation and interlibrary loans, also lend themselves to counting, codifying, and evaluating the quantity and sometimes the quality of the product. It has taken much longer to evaluate any reference services, because it is not easy to evaluate human interaction. Nevertheless, evaluation is recommended in the American Library Association guidelines, which state:

> The library should appraise the performance of individual informa-
> tion service staff members and of the collective performance of that
> staff at regular intervals, using recognized personnel evaluation
> techniques and instruments agreed to in advance by those to be
> evaluated and those performing the evaluation.[1]

95

The performance of one person during human interaction is what must be evaluated during the reference interview. "There is no doubt that it is inherently difficult to assess an activity that has interpersonal communication as its basis."[2] Evaluation of the reference interview varies from evaluation of reference service in general to evaluations that try to determine the accuracy of reference answers. This discussion concerns the evaluation of a librarian's *communication skills* during the interview, which are an essential part of the total performance picture.

Edward Evans states, in *Management Techniques for Librarians,* that evaluation has two forms: daily, informal comments and periodic, written evaluation.[3] Both are important. To evaluate a staff member only periodically, with no comments whatsoever about performance between evaluations, does nothing to reinforce good performance, bolster professional satisfaction, or indicate that performance is not as good as it should be. Evaluating only periodically, without some informal comments in between, can take staff members by surprise, especially if they are unaware that they have any performance problems whatsoever.

Why evaluate at all? In some cases evaluations have been instituted in response to employment legalities. Employers are acutely aware of the constant possibility of litigation about employment practices. Rather than developing evaluation procedures as a positive response to the need for the best performance possible from each staff member, some evaluation is no more than a defense mechanism against the possibility that a disgruntled employee may sue. Also, in systems or institutions where salary increases are tied only to the cost of living or other outside factors, evaluation may not relate in any way to monetary remuneration—in these cases, evaluation, like virtue, is its own reward. Sometimes good performance receives no more reward than mediocre performance. In fact, good performance often means added responsibilities and duties. But as professionals, librarians recognize the value of evaluation and strive to include it in their professional lives.

Evaluation can yield many benefits. It gives supervisors and managers a structured way, no matter how informal, to evaluate staff and to motivate staff to improve performance. For the librarian with serious performance deficiencies, it can lead to continuing education and definite improvement in performance. If evaluation leads to dismissal, the entire organization may thereby be improved. For the individual, nothing is more gratifying than a positive evaluation to bolster morale and reinforce the commitment to the best possible performance.

The atmosphere in which evaluation takes place is critical. In many ways evaluation is easier in small libraries than in large facilities, because all staff members work closely with one another every day. It quickly becomes obvious where deficiencies lie or where improvements can be made. The manager, supervisor, or director in a small setting has ample opportunities to evaluate frequently and informally; almost daily, in fact. Generally, staff members have a good idea where they stand before formal, periodic evaluations are conducted.

There are several situations in small facilities in which evaluation can be a problem, in terms of who evaluates a librarian. In a special library, for example, the librarian working alone may be evaluated by someone who is not a librarian and may or may not be clear about standards of service and specific performance quality factors. The same may be true of school or public libraries. In larger settings, librarians may be evaluated by other library professionals who do not see their performance on a daily basis and therefore rely on general impressions or written evaluations from others.

Why bother at all? Because, as professionals, librarians believe a strong evaluation program is important to the provision of excellent services to patrons. The following are some of the benefits of a performance evaluation program, according to Robert Stueart and Barbara Moran.

1. Systematic, written performance appraisal provides a method of distinguishing among the performance of employees.

2. Appraisal determines how well an employee performs.

3. It helps employees to know where improvement is needed and where they are doing well.

4. Appraisal can be the basis for personnel decisions (promotion, demotion, etc.) and salary decisions.

5. Appraisal helps employees to establish personal goals.

6. Appraisal can facilitate better understanding between employees and supervisors.[4]

Any standard personnel management text will provide more reasons to have an evaluation program in place. It is a foregone conclusion in most organizations that some sort of evaluation will take place, whether formalized or not. Regardless of whether evaluations are done for idealistic, professional reasons; as defense mechanisms; or for accountability in an era of budget constraints, good evaluation can only have a positive effect on the profession as a whole. One of the important factors in evaluation is that it should be accepted as a fact of professional life.

Several other factors contribute to a positive atmosphere in which evaluation can be conducted. Guidelines under which a reference librarian is to be evaluated should be as specific as possible. "[I]t is possible to conduct effective and meaningful evaluations of reference interview practice if each study carefully determines exactly what, and in what terms, is being examined."[5] A librarian should know how he or she will be evaluated, under what conditions, by whom, and how those evaluations will be reported. It hardly makes for good staff morale if everyone is evaluated differently and by different criteria.

One example of specific performance standards being developed by an academic reference department has been reported by Carole Larson and Laura Dickson. Two broad goals were developed: first, that staff at the reference desk should relate positively to patrons; second, that staff should be responsible and dependable coworkers. The list of observable behaviors that show that a librarian is interacting positively with patrons includes both verbal and nonverbal behaviors. Among the behaviors that encourage patrons to ask questions are

- Smiling
- Making positive eye contact
- Listening before commenting
- Stopping work at the desk to help patrons
- Remaining calm when dealing with patrons[6]

The performance standards were used for self-evaluation as well as performance evaluation. An additional use was for training new personnel, because "[t]he standards provide the trainee with a concrete list of satisfactory performance behaviors, and serve as a catalyst for discussion between the trainer and trainee regarding values and expectations."[7]

METHODS TO EVALUATE THE INTERVIEW

Evaluation of a reference interview requires specific guidelines, as does any other evaluation. The appraisals can be done in a number of ways, the most effective of which is observation through the use of videotaping. What makes this type of observation so effective is that not only does the evaluator have a chance to observe the reference librarian, but also the librarian can see his or her own performance on tape. As documented by Judith Mucci, there are a number of ways to do the actual taping, and librarians on the job can probably come up with even more imaginative ways.[8] During taping for evaluation, the patrons should be taken into account and their right to refuse to be taped honored. A sign posted at the reference service point indicating the times during which taping will be done alerts patrons so they can refuse to be taped if they wish. Generally, patrons do not mind, particularly if better service is the ultimate goal. Only a representative sample of interviews need be taped. One of the benefits of seeing oneself on videotape is that bad or distracting habits almost jump off the screen. The evaluation of the videotape can be done in a number of ways. It can be viewed by the supervisor and librarian together so that they can discuss various skills and performance. Tapes can also be viewed in a group setting where all reference librarians view all the tapes and discuss problems, ways to improve, and so on. In either case, the librarian being taped should have the final word on who is to see the tape.

Before the interview evaluation takes place, everyone involved should know what skills are being assessed and why. In other words, guidelines should be set up. The guidelines could be a list of the skills that should be demonstrated during the interview. This is the most comprehensive way to look at the interview and to evaluate it. It also enables the librarian and the manager to look for skills that are performed well and those that need improvement. Sometimes when librarians first begin the evaluation of interviews, they do not evaluate specific skills, but start by looking for general attributes in the interview. This can be a good way to start if the library staff has never tried to look at interviews on tape before. Some of the general attributes that can be evaluated are professional appearance and demeanor; positive, pleasant attitude; and the ability to find out what information the patron really needs.

To evaluate the total interview, a number of factors must be taken into account. With so many factors, it is advisable to try to evaluate only a few at a time. Tracy Bicknell delineates factors that can be taken into account when assessing the quality of reference services:

- User needs and expectations

- Behavior and communication skills of librarian

- Environment: physical and service

- Morale[9]

The problem with only looking at general attitudes is that the evaluation can become too subjective. Trying to pinpoint specific interviewing skills can lead to more objective and effective evaluations. "The emphasis throughout the analysis should be not only on judging the goodness or badness of a group of interviews or an individual's performance in interviewing, but also on identifying the elements within the interview that contribute to the assessment."[10] David Tyckoson states that:

> To avoid gross generalizations, methods that evaluate behavior must break down that behavior into its component parts. By measuring incremental features of the librarian's behavior, the evaluator will be able to make more objective judgments and the librarian being evaluated will receive feedback that may be used to improve specific aspects of his/her performance.[11]

Roma Harris and Gillian Michell conducted two studies using videotaped interviews. For their studies, they hired professional actors who used a script and taped reference interviews. The tapes were then shown to a sample of public library patrons in the first study[12] and to a sample of librarians in the second study.[13] The interviews were evaluated on three aspects:

- Nonverbal warmth shown toward the patron. A high-warmth condition was exhibited through smiling, eye contact, warm voice tone, and open body posture. A low-warmth condition was exhibited by a more neutral level of warmth.

- Inclusion. "By this we are referring to the degree to which the professional librarian instructs or educates the user about the process of using library resources to answer a reference question and, by doing so, includes the patron in the reference process."[14]

Both librarians and patrons who evaluated the tapes gave the highest competence ratings to the reference librarians who showed high-level warmth. In summary, Michell and Harris reported that "patrons and professionals are alike in finding reference performance more competent when accompanied by nonverbal warmth."[15] They also found that professional librarians are more critical of overall competence than are library patrons.

Although the reference interview should be emphasized, it will be only one of the factors used in a total evaluation of an individual librarian. What is important about this part of the evaluation is that, if conducted by assessing specific interviewing skills, it is easier to improve performance than if only general attitudes are assessed.

So far, the only method of evaluating interviews we have mentioned is videotaping. There are other ways. The use of audiotapes can be highly successful to evaluate verbal behaviors. Audiocassette players are even more unobtrusive than video equipment, and the reference librarian can turn the tape on at the start of the interview. Audiotapes permit listening specifically for evidence of verbal behaviors, such as asking open questions, closing, summarizing content, and the like. Voice-activated recording devices are an effective means of taping interviews.

A number of studies have used audiotaping as a means of evaluating interviews. Dewdney provides an extensive report of her work in *Qualitative Research in Information Management* (discussed in chapter 3).[16] As with videotaping, patrons must know they are being taped and give prior consent.

Marilyn Von Seggern reported on a study that used a microcassette recorder carried in a pocket with a tie-clip microphone attached to the lapel. Using a combination of librarians listening to and commenting on their tapes, an assessment instrument developed by Murfin and Gugelchuk, and observer notes, Von Seggern assisted librarians in evaluating their performance. One of the drawbacks of this method was that it was too intrusive and time-consuming to be used frequently for evaluation, although it was useful on an occasional basis. Results included the following:

- The use of questions facilitated successful question negotiation.

- Certain reference policies were called into question.

- Librarians recognized that improvement of interviewing skills is a continuous process.[17]

Another method of observing the interview is to have one person observe the interview *and* make notes on specific behaviors. This is difficult to do, particularly the first time one tries it. One librarian or supervisor can observe another's interviews over the course of time to pick up patterns of behavior and the use of various verbal and nonverbal skills. Not only is this method more time-consuming, it is less effective than using video- or audiotaping. The one advantage this method has is that the observer can follow the librarian and the patron when the interview becomes mobile. Any reference librarian knows that after the initial interview takes place, the majority of interviews continue either while using specific tools or while directing the patron to another part of the library. Reference librarians move away from the reference service point constantly, and it is difficult to follow along and take notes on behaviors in all the places the interview might take the patron and the librarian.

The patron is obviously a critical element in the evaluation of the interview. It is not always necessary, however, to question the patron about his or her satisfaction with the interview. In any observation, whether by taping or personal observation, one can often discern whether the patron is happy with the outcome of the interview. In fact, patrons are often pleased with the interview even if their questions cannot be or were not answered.

It is not necessary to use real-life situations to evaluate interviews. Just as the interviews are staged when teaching interviewing skills in the classroom, so interviews can be staged in the workplace. Staff members can role-play the parts of patrons, or several patrons could be invited to come ask questions at specific times. This last procedure of asking for volunteers among actual library patrons is particularly successful in school and academic settings. Students will often be amenable to lending a hand. (College drama classes are particularly good places to find volunteers.) One should not worry about staging interviews. If the questions are serious, the reference librarian soon forgets about the staging. Role-playing interviews are an excellent alternative in settings where taping during normal service hours is quite impractical.

Tracy Bicknell, in an article in the *Journal of Academic Librarianship*, gives an excellent summary of the ways to measure communication skills and behaviors. These strategies include

- Customized skill assessment (CSA) developed in-house

- Peer evaluation related to performance improvement

- Evaluation based on objectives, content, and form of the interview, as well as the end product

- A rating scale whereby staff set goals to improve their own performance

- A Reference Transaction Assessment Instrument (RTAI)

- A panel of experts to evaluate interviews, along with a model such as the Attributive Quality Theory[18]

Any reference unit that desires to improve performance in the reference interview should look at such strategies, along with others, to ascertain the most appropriate and feasible methodology.

Any number of configurations can be used to observe and evaluate the interview. Table 10-1 on page 102 is modified from an article by Marilyn White on evaluating the interview. It shows some of the possibilities and combinations that can be used to evaluate interviews.[19]

There is no standard form to use when evaluating interviewing skills. Some models are available, or a library can adapt or create its own form. Two forms that currently exist are the one in table 3-1 on page 31, which lists the interviewing skills and permits rating of each of those skills, and the Model Reference Behaviors

Table 10-1. Interview Evaluations

OBSERVER CAN BE:	Self
	Peer
	Supervisor
	Outside expert
NATURE OF	Real
INTERVIEWS	Staged obtrusively
CAN BE:	Staged unobtrusively
INTERVIEWS CAN	By videotape
BE OBSERVED:	By audiotape
	In person
	By combination of recorded and personal observation

Checklist, which was used in a study of reference performance in Maryland public libraries.[20] The actual form used is not as important as having the evaluation form, if one is used, be simple and straightforward. Table 10-2 lists questions that should be asked when setting up an evaluation procedure for interviewing skills.

Evaluation is time-consuming and difficult. It takes cooperation and flexibility on all sides. However, the results in higher esteem, better performance, and clearer understanding of communication skills are well worth the effort.

Table 10-2. Interviewing Evaluation Checklist

_____ Why do we want to evaluate reference interview skills?

_____ What kind of observation will we use?

Video _____ Audio _____

Personal observation _____

Combination _____

_____ Who will observe?

_____ Who will view recorded interviews?

_____ Exactly what skills are we looking for?

_____ Are we planning to use an evaluation form?

_____ Will we use real or staged interviews?

_____ Who will we use as patrons if staged?

_____ How will the results of the evaluation be used?

NOTES

[1]Bryce Allen, "Evaluation of Reference Services," in *Reference and Information Services*, ed. Richard E. Bopp and Linda C. Smith (Englewood, CO: Libraries Unlimited, 1991), 265.

[2]Lisa L. Smith, "Evaluating the Reference Interview: A Theoretical Discussion of the Desirability and Achievability of Evaluation," *RQ* 31 (fall 1991): 77.

[3]G. Edward Evans, *Management Techniques for Librarians* (New York: Academic Press, 1976), 202.

[4]Robert D. Stueart and Barbara B. Moran, *Library and Information Center Management*, 4th ed. (Englewood, CO: Libraries Unlimited, 1993), 147–48.

[5]Smith, "Evaluating the Reference Interview," 78.

[6]Carole A. Larson and Laura K. Dickson, "Developing Behavioral Reference Desk Performance Standards," *RQ* 33 (spring 1994): 353.

[7]Ibid.

[8]Judith Mucci, "Videotape Self-Evaluation in Public Libraries: Experiments in Evaluating Public Services," *RQ* 16 (fall 1976): 33–37.

[9]Tracy Bicknell, "Focusing on Quality Reference Service," *Journal of Academic Librarianship* 20 (May 1994): 77.

[10]Marilyn Domas White, "Evaluation of the Reference Interview," *RQ* 25 (fall 1985): 83.

[11]David A. Tyckoson, "Wrong Questions, Wrong Answers: Behavioral vs. Factual Evaluation of Reference Service," *Reference Librarian*, no. 38 (1992): 167.

[12]Roma M. Harris and B. Gillian Michell, "The Social Context of Reference Work: Assessing the Effects of Gender and Communication Skill on Observers' Judgments and Competence," *Library and Information Science Research* 8 (January 1986): 85–101.

[13]Gillian Michell and Roma M. Harris, "Evaluating the Reference Interview: Some Factors Influencing Patrons and Professionals," *RQ* 27 (fall 1987): 95–105.

[14]Ibid., 104.

[15]Ibid.

[16]Patricia Dewdney, "Recording the Reference Interview: A Field Experiment," in *Qualitative Research in Information Management*, ed. Jack D. Glazier and Ronald R. Powell (Englewood, CO: Libraries Unlimited, 1992).

[17]Marilyn Vor Zeggern, "Evaluating the Interview," *RQ* 29 (winter 1989): 263–64.

[18]Bicknell, "Focusing on Quality Reference Service," 79.

[19]White, "Evaluation of the Reference Interview," 79.

[20]Ralph Gers and Lillie J. Seward, "Improving Reference Performance: Results of a Statewide Study," *Library Journal 110* (November 1, 1985): 34.

11

Finale

As the curtain comes down on this discussion of the reference interview, there are some final thoughts and observations to be made. A main point to remember is that no improvement in the reference interview can be made unless a librarian or paraprofessional is committed to the idea of the interview as an integral part of communication. Without that commitment, there is a lack of motivation for improving and continuing to improve skills.

In each chapter, we have tried to give some practical advice about the reference interview and the particular topic under discussion. A central part of our mission has been to clarify the process of communication during the interview. Of course, some people are more adept at communicating than others, but everyone can benefit from improving a specific set of skills.

The 12 interviewing skills delineated in the book have proven to be the basic building blocks of communication in the interview. The work of Allen Ivey, upon which our original research was based, has flourished not only in the area of counseling, but also in a number of other fields, including library science.

EFFECT OF TECHNOLOGY

The tremendous effect of technology on reference service has served to highlight the importance of an effective reference interview with patrons. Sophisticated searching tools, myriad databases, Internet access, CD-ROMs, and other technologies have been added to traditional resources at an astounding rate. An effective interview ensures that the patron's real information need is met through use of the most appropriate resources.

Along with technology to access information, librarians and staff have technological tools that facilitate but also escalate avenues of communication. From voicemail to e-mail to interactive media, library staff can receive and send messages many ways, and thus must use interpersonal skills in novel and creative ways.

PROFESSIONAL GUIDELINES AND EVALUATION

Librarians now have various guidelines, produced by divisions of ALA, that validate and emphasize the need for excellent interviewing skills. Of singular importance are the *Guidelines for Behavioral Evaluation of Reference and Information Services Performance* which, when combined with more sophisticated evaluation techniques, give librarians a much firmer foundation in evaluating verbal and nonverbal skills and the interview in general. The evaluation of interpersonal skills has seen dramatic advances in a number of disciplines, many of which may be applied to the reference interview. It is hoped that further efforts will be made to use recent techniques in the study and analysis of library encounters.

TQM AND CUSTOMER SERVICE

Although *TQM* and *customer service* have become rather hackneyed terms, the training materials and concepts from the quality movement are extremely useful for librarians. Videos, audiocassettes, training manuals, and other materials can be adapted readily to library service. The concepts and training elements are very basic, but they can provide a solid foundation for discussions and improvement of service to library users. More is also known now about videotaping situations to promote and evaluate customer service situations.

SPECIAL POPULATIONS

In recent years, a new and pervasive awareness of the special populations who use libraries has grown tremendously. With the passage of the ADA, the growth of the immigrant and elderly populations, and the increased fears for personal safety, the literature of librarianship provides more help, ideas, and advice concerning these matters than it did even a decade ago. The use of interpersonal skills is critical for dealing effectively and in a caring manner with special populations.

IN CLOSING

One of the disservices reference librarians sometimes do to themselves is to refer to the interview only as art. Art, drama, and other creative endeavors all have techniques that must be mastered. After those techniques have been mastered, the artist is able to add style, personality, and other unique attributes to the final creation. So it is with the reference interview. It is an art, but one that requires the use of specific skills. Creative and successful use of these skills contributes to the art of the interview.

The reference interview must also be viewed in the full context of public services. A good reference interview is a keystone of service, but other skills must also be present to round out the picture. For example, without a thorough knowledge of reference tools available in a particular collection, it is very difficult for the librarian to follow up and find the information a patron wants. By the same token, a reference librarian should have a thorough knowledge of the library, its staff, its policies, and its procedures. The library profession spends a great deal of time networking and standardizing practices as much as possible, but the number of unique local practices that abound is amazing. Consequently, even the most seasoned librarian will feel like a rookie when placed in a new environment. The general environment of a library must be one of helpfulness if it is to support the service efforts of the librarians dealing directly with patrons. The reference interview is part of a larger picture of professionalism that must be present if service is to succeed.

In closing, it is hoped that this book will stimulate discussion and further study of the interview and that it will be used in many of the following ways:

- To integrate the interview further into library science curricula

- To obtain ideas for staff training and development through use of customer service materials and techniques

- To learn specific interviewing skills

- To gain some insight into working with special patrons

- To examine the physical setting in which reference service takes place

- To consider the effect of technology on reference encounters

- To become aware of all the possible places where interviews are conducted, even when not in public services

- To consider and develop policies for events that take place around the interview (e.g., telephone service, e-mail service, etc.)

- To teach and evaluate more effectively the interviewing skills of public services staff

The most important use of the information contained herein should be to improve service to library patrons. The ultimate goal of any library is to provide the best possible service. Good service must rely heavily on the successful interview between patron and librarian. It is the duty of librarians to set the stage and to use the appropriate acting techniques—that is, communication skills—to please the audience.

Bibliography

Abels, Eileen G. "The E-mail Reference Interview." *RQ* 35 (spring 1996): 345–58.

Alberico, Ralph. "Minimalist Approach to CD-ROM Instruction." *Lifeline* 44 (fall 1990): 1–3.

Allegri, Francesca. "On the Other Side of the Reference Desk: The Patron with a Physical Disability." *Medical Reference Services Quarterly* 3 (fall 1984): 65–76.

Allen, Bryce. "Evaluation of Reference Services." In *Reference and Information Services,* edited by Richard E. Bopp and Linda C. Smith. Englewood, CO: Libraries Unlimited, 1991.

Allen, Gillian. "CD-ROM Training: What Do the Patrons Want?" *RQ* 30 (fall 1990): 88–93.

Allen, Gillian, and Bryce Allen. "Service Orientation as a Selection Criterion for Public Service Librarians." *Journal of Library Administration* 16, no. 4 (1992): 67–77.

Allen, Mary Beth. "International Students in Academic Libraries: A User Survey." *College and Research Libraries* 54 (July 1993): 323–33.

Allen, Melody Lloyd. "Talking with Young Children in the Library." *American Libraries* (October 1989): 926–28.

Allerton, Mark. "Am I Asking the Right Questions? (What Teachers Ask of Children)." *International Journal of Early Childhood* 25, no. 1 (1992): 42–48.

Alloway, Catherine Suyak. "The Courteous Librarian: Helping Public Service Employees to Keep Smiling." *Reference Librarian* 16 (winter 1986): 283–96.

Aluri, Rao. "Improving Reference Service: The Case for Using a Continuous Quality Improvement Method." *Reference Librarian* 16 (winter 1986): 220–36.

And Access for All: *ADA and Your Library*. Chicago: American Library Association Video 1993. (Guide originally compiled by the State Library of Florida) (video, 47 min.; 167-page guide).

Anderson, A. J. "Can Store Service Policy Fit a Library?" *Library Journal* 115 (November 1, 1990): 64–66.

Anderson, Byron, and Samuel T. Huang. "Impact of New Library Technology on Training Paraprofessional Staff." *Reference Librarian*, no. 39 (1993): 21–29.

Anderson, Charles. "Reference Anxiety." *RQ* 30 (winter 1990): 173–74 (part of "The Exchange" column).

Arthur, Gwen. "Customer-Service Training in Academic Libraries." *Journal of Academic Librarianship* 20 (September 1994): 219–22.

Barbuto, Domenica M., and Elena E. Cevallos. "The Delivery of Reference Services in a CD-ROM LAN Environment: A Case Study." *RQ* 34 (fall 1994): 60–76.

Bazillion, Richard, and Connie Braun. A*cademic Libraries as High-Tech Gateways: A Guide to Design and Space Decisions.* Chicago: American Library Association, 1995.

Benham, Frances, and Ronald R. Powell. *Success in Answering Reference Questions: Two Studies.* Metuchen, NJ: Scarecrow Press, 1987.

Benson, Larry D., and H. Julene Butler. "Reference Philosophy vs. Service Reality." *Reference Librarian* 12 (spring/summer 1985): 83–91.

Bergen, Kathleen, and Barbara MacAdam. "One-on-One: Term Paper Assistance Programs." *RQ* 24 (spring 1985): 333–40.

Berger, Gilda. *Speech and Language Disorders.* New York: Franklin Watts, 1981.

Bessler, Joanne M. *Putting Service into Library Staff Training.* Chicago: American Library Association, 1994.

Bicknell, Tracy. "Focusing on Quality Reference Service." *Journal of Academic Librarianship* 20 (May 1994): 77–81.

Birch, Nancy, Maurice P. Marchant, and Nathan M. Smith. "Perceived Role Conflict, Role Ambiguity, and Reference Librarian Burnout in Public Libraries." *Library and Information Science Research* 8 (January/March 1986): 53–65.

Black, William K., guest ed. "Libraries and Student Assistants: Critical Links." *Journal of Library Administration* 21, no. 3/4 (1995).

Blazek, Ron, and Darlene Ann Parrish. "Burnout and Public Services: The Periodical Literature of Librarianship in the Eighties." *RQ* 31 (fall 1992): 48–59.

Bone, Diane. *The Business of Listening: A Practical Guide to Effective Listening.* Menlo Park, CA: Crisp Publications, 1988.

Boone, Morrell D., Sandra G. Yee, and Rita Bullard. *Training Student Library Assistants.* Chicago: American Library Association, 1991.

Boucher, Virginia. "The Interlibrary Loan Interview." *Reference Librarian* 16 (winter 1986): 89–95.

———. "Nonverbal Communication and the Library Reference Interview." *RQ* 16 (fall 1976): 27–32.

"Brief Encounters: Using Techniques from Psychology and Education to Improve the Effectiveness of Reference Service." ACRL/Chicago, 1992. Educational and Behavioral Services Section. Handouts from the Conference Program, San Francisco, CA: June 27–July 2, 1992.

Brinkman, Rick, and Rick Kirschner. "How to Deal with Difficult People." Audiocassette seminar. Boulder, CO: CareerTrack Publications, 1987.

Brown, Carol R. "Service Desks." In *Planning Library Interiors.* Phoenix, AZ: Oryx Press, 1995.

Bryant, Sue Lacey. *Personal Professional Development and the Solo Librarian*. London: Library Association, 1995.

Budd, John M. *The Library and Its Users: The Communication Process*. New York: Greenwood Press, 1992.

Bunge, Charles A. "Interpersonal Dimensions of the Interview: A Historical Review of the Literature." *Drexel Library Quarterly* 20 (spring 1984): 4–23.

———. "Potential and Reality at the Reference Desk: Reflections on 'Return to the Field.'" *Journal of Academic Librarianship* 10 (July 1984): 128–32.

———. "Responsive Reference Service: Breaking Down Age Barriers." *School Library Journal* 40 (March 1994): 142–45.

———. "Stress in the Library." *Library Journal* 112, no. 15 (September 15, 1987): 47–51.

Callaghan, Linda Ward. "Children's Questions: Reference Interviews with the Young." *Reference Librarian* 7/8 (spring/summer 1983): 55–65.

Cargill, Jennifer. "The Electronic Reference Desk: Reference Service in an Electronic World." *Library Administration and Management* 6 (spring 1992): 82–85.

Cassidy, Deborah J. "Questioning the Young Child: Process and Function." *Childhood Education* 65 (spring 1989): 146–49.

Champlin, Peggy. "The Online Search: Some Perils and Pitfalls." *RQ* 25 (winter 1985): 213–17.

Chancellor, John, Miriam D. Tompkins, and Hazel I. Medway. *Helping the Reader Toward Self-Education*. Chicago: American Library Association, 1938.

Cheney, Frances Neel, and Wiley J. Williams. *Fundamental Reference Sources*. 2d ed. Chicago: American Library Association, 1980.

Coleman, Kathleen, and Elizabeth Magitti. "Training Nonprofessionals for Reference Service." *RQ* 16 (spring 1977): 217–19.

"Communicating and Interacting with People Who Have Disabilities." Equal Employment Opportunity Commission, 1994 (60p.).

Condic, Kristine Salomon. "Reference Assistance for CD-ROM Users: A Little Goes a Long Way." *CD-ROM Professional* 5 (January 1992): 56–57.

Conroy, Barbara, and Barbara Schindler Jones. *Improving Communication in the Library*. Phoenix, AZ: Oryx Press, 1986.

Controlling the Confrontation: Arch Lustberg on Effective Communication Techniques. Towson, MD: ALA Video/Video Library Network (videocassette, 44 min.).

Courtois, Martin P. "Use of Nonprofessionals at Reference Desks." *College and Research Libraries* 45 (September 1984): 385–91.

Craver, Kathleen W. "Bridging the Gap: Library Services for Immigrant Populations." *Journal of Youth Services in Libraries* 4 (winter 1991): 123–30.

Crispen, Joanne L., ed. *The Americans with Disabilities Act: Its Impact on Libraries*. ALA Association of Specialized and Cooperative Library Agencies Preconference. San Francisco, June 26, 1992. Chicago: ASCLA, 1993.

Crook, Joyce M. "Designing the Perfect Reference Desk." *Library Journal* 108 (May 1983): 970–72.

Crosson, Vicky L. "Hey! Kids Are Patrons, Too!" *Texas Libraries* 52 (summer 1991): 48–50.

Customer Service—More Than a Smile. Towson, MD: ALA Video/Library Video Network, 1991 (videocassette, 13 min.).

Dalrymple, Prudence W. "Closing the Gap: The Role of the Librarian in Online Searching." *RQ* 24 (winter 1984): 177–83.

Decker, Bert. *The Art of Communicating*. Los Altos, CA: Crisp Publications, 1988.

Del Vecchio, Rosemary A. "Privacy and Accountability at the Reference Desk." *Reference Librarian* no. 38 (1992): 133–40.

Dequin, Henry, Irene Schilling, and Samuel Huang. "The Attitudes of Academic Librarians Toward Disabled Persons." *Journal of Academic Librarianship* 14, no. 1 (1988): 28–31.

Dervin, Brenda, and Patricia Dewdney. "Neutral Questioning: A New Approach to the Reference Interview." *RQ* 25 (summer 1986): 506–13.

DeVore-Chew, Marynelle, Brian Roberts, and Nathan M. Smith. "The Effects of Reference Librarians' Nonverbal Communications on the Patrons' Perceptions of the Library, Librarians, and Themselves." *Library and Information Science Research* 10 (October–December 1988): 389–400.

Dewdney, Patricia. "Recording the Reference Interview: A Field Experiment." In *Qualitative Research in Information Management*, edited by Jack D. Glazier and Ronald R. Powell. Englewood, CO: Libraries Unlimited, 1992.

Dewdney, Patricia, and Catherine Sheldrick Ross. "Flying a Light Aircraft: Reference Service Evaluation from a User's Viewpoint." *RQ* 34 (winter 1994): 217–30.

The Difficult Reference Question. Chicago: ALA Video, 1986 (videocassette, 19 min.).

"Does This Answer Your Question?" Baltimore, MD: Library Video Network, 1985 (videocassette, 16 min.).

Does This Completely Answer Your Question? Chicago: ALA Video, 1992 (videocassette, 19 min.).

Dowler, Larry. "Our Edifice at the Precipice." *Library Journal* 121 (February 15, 1996): 118–20.

Durrance, Joan C. "Reference Success: Does the 55 Percent Rule Tell the Whole Story?" *Library Journal* 114 (April 15, 1989): 31–36.

Eberhart, George M., comp. *The Whole Library Handbook 2*. Chicago: American Library Association, 1992.

Edmonds, Leslie, and Ellen D. Sutton. "The Reference Interview." In *Reference and Information Services*, edited by Richard E. Bopp and Linda C. Smith. Englewood, CO: Libraries Unlimited, 1991.

Eichman, Thomas Lee. "The Complex Nature of Opening Reference Questions." *RQ* 17 (spring 1978): 212–22.

Ellison, J. W., and C. Molenda. "Making Yourself Approachable." *New Library World* 77 (November 1976): 214–15.

Emmick, Nancy. "Nonprofessionals on Reference Desks in Academic Libraries." *Reference Librarian* 12 (spring/summer 1985): 149–60.

The End of the Line. Des Moines, IA: American Media, 1992 (videocassette, 15 min.; training leader's guide).

Evans, Anita K. "Electronic Reference Services: Mediation for the 1990s." *Reference Librarian* no. 37 (1992): 75–86.

Evans, G. Edward. *Management Techniques for Librarians*. New York: Academic Press, 1976.

Evans, G. Edward, Anthony J. Amodeo, and Thomas L. Carter. *Introduction to Library Public Services*. Library Science Text Series. Englewood, CO: Libraries Unlimited, 1992.

Ewing, Keith, and Robert Hauptman. "Is Traditional Reference Service Obsolete?" *Journal of Academic Librarianship* 21 (January 1995): 3–6.

Fairbairn, Donald. "The Art of Questioning Your Students." *Clearing House* 61 (September 1987): 19–22.

Fast, Julius. *Body Language*. New York: Pocket Books, 1982.

Ferguson, Chris. "Reshaping Academic Library Reference Service." *Advances in Librarianship* 18 (1994): 73–109.

Figueroa, J. Degado. *Training for Non-Trainers: A Practical Guide*. Amherst, MA: HRD Press, 1994.

Fimian, Michael J., et al. "The Measure of Occupational Stress and Burnout among Library Medical Specialists." *Library and Information Science Research* 11 (January–March 1989): 3–19.

Fine, Sara. "Reference and Resources: The Human Side." *Journal of Academic Librarianship* 21 (January 1995): 17–25.

Flexner, Jennie M., and Sigrid A. Edge. *A Reader's Advisory Service*. New York: American Association for Adult Education, 1934.

Flexner, Jennie M., and Byron C. Hopkins. *Reader's Advisors at Work*. New York: American Association for Adult Education, 1941.

Foos, Donald D., and Nancy C. Pack. *How Libraries Must Comply with the Americans with Disabilities Act (ADA)*. Phoenix, AZ: Oryx Press, 1992.

Frank, Donald. "Management of Student Assistants in a Public Services Setting of an Academic Library." *RQ* 24 (fall 1984): 51–57.

Futas, Elizabeth. "Current Issues in Reference and Adult Services." *RQ* 29 (spring 1990): 328–31.

Gavryck, Jacquelyn. "Library Instruction for Clerical Staff: The Rest of the Iceberg." *Journal of Academic Librarianship* 11 (January 1986): 343–45.

Gers, Ralph, and Lillie J. Seward. " 'I Heard You Say . . .' Peer Coaching for More Effective Reference Service." *Reference Librarian*, no. 22 (1988): 245–60.

———. "Improving Reference Performance: Results of a Statewide Study." *Library Journal* 110 (November 1, 1985): 32–35.

Glazier, Jack. "Structured Observation: How It Works." *College and Research Libraries News* 46 (March 1985): 105–8.

Glogoff, Stuart. "Communication Theory's Role in the Reference Interview." *Drexel Library Quarterly* 19 (spring 1983): 56–72.

Goetsch, Lori. "Reference Service Is More Than a Desk." *Journal of Academic Librarianship* 21 (January 1995): 15–16.

Goldmann, Warren R., and James R. Mallory. "Overcoming Communication Barriers." *Library Trends* 40 (summer 1992): 21–30.

Gothberg, Helen M. "The Beginnings." *Reference Librarian* 16 (winter 1986): 7–17.

Greenfield, Louise, Susan Johnston, and Karen Williams. "Educating the World: Training Library Staff to Communicate Effectively with International Students." *Journal of Academic Librarianship* 12 (September 1986): 227–31.

Groark, James L. "Assertion: A Technique for Handling Troublesome Library Patrons." *Catholic Library World* 51 (November 1979): 172–75.

Grochmal, Helen M. "The Serials Department's Responsibilities for Reference." *RQ* 20 (summer 1981): 403–6.

Grosser, Kerry. "Burnout Amongst Librarians and Information Workers." *LASIE* 18 (September/October 1987): 32–41.

"Guidelines for Multilingual Materials Collection and Development and Library Services." *RQ* 30 (winter 1990): 268–71.

Habich, Elizabeth C. "Effective and Efficient Library Space Planning and Design." In *Operations Handbook for the Small Academic Library*, edited by Gerard B. McCabe. New York: Greenwood Press, 1989.

Hales-Mabry, Celia. "Serving the Older Adult." *Reference Librarian*, no. 31 (1991): 69–76.

Hall, Edward T. *The Silent Language*. Garden City, NY: Doubleday, 1959.

Halldorsson, Egill A., and Marjorie E. Murfin. "The Performance of Professionals and Nonprofessionals in the Reference Interview." *College and Research Libraries* 38 (September 1977): 385–95.

Hammond, Carol. "Information and Research Support Services: The Reference Librarian and the Information Paraprofessional." *Reference Librarian*, no. 37 (1992): 91–104.

Harris, Roma M., and B. Gillian Michell. "The Social Context of Reference Work: Assessing the Effects of Gender and Communication Skill on Observers' Judgments and Competence." *Library and Information Science Research* 8 (January 1986): 85–101.

Hauptman, Robert. "The Myth of the Reference Interview." *Reference Librarian* 16 (winter 1986): 47–52.

Hendrickson, Linnea. "Deskless Reference Services." *Catholic Library World* 55 (September 1983): 81–84.

Hensley, Randall. "Learning Style Theory and Learning Transfer Principles During Reference Interview Instruction." *Library Trends* 39 (winter 1991): 203–9.

Hicks, Jack Alan. "Mediation in Reference Service to Extend Patron Success." *Reference Librarian*, no. 37 (1992): 49–64.

Hiebing, Dottie. "Current Trends in the Continuing Education and Training of Reference Staff." *Reference Librarian*, no. 30 (winter 1990): 5–15.

Holland, Barron. "Updating Library Reference Services Through Training for Interpersonal Competence." *RQ* 17 (spring 1978): 207–11.

Horning, Kathleen T. "Fishing for Questions (Library Reference Work with Children)." *Wilson Library Bulletin* 68 (May 1994): 57–59.

———. "How Can I Help You? The Joys and Challenges of Reference Work with Children." *Show-Me-Libraries* 45 (spring/summer 1994): 9–19.

Horswill, Diane. "What Can You Do with a Hostile Client?" Seattle, WA: Crime Prevention Division, Seattle Police Department, 1994 (brochure).

Howell, Benita J., et al. "Fleeting Encounters: A Role Analysis of Reference Librarian-Patron Interaction." *RQ* 16 (winter 1976): 124–29.

Humphries, Anne Wood. "Designing a Functional Reference Desk: Planning to Completion." *RQ* 33 (fall 1993): 35–40.

Hurych, Jitka. "The Professional and the Client: The Reference Interview Revisited." *Reference Librarian* 5/6 (fall/winter 1982): 199–205.

If It Weren't for the Patron. Chicago: ALA Video, 1988. Directed by Jeff Lifton (videocassette, 17 min.).

"If It Weren't for the Patron—Evaluating Your Public Service Attitude." Baltimore, MD: Library Video Network, 1981 (videocassette [½ or ¾ inch], 18 min.).

" 'In My Judgment . . .' An Informal Discussion of the Future of Reference Services." *Reference Librarian* (fall/winter 1981): 131–86.

"Information Services for Information Consumers: Guidelines for Providers." *RQ* 30 (winter 1990): 262–65.

Irving, Suzanne. "Addressing the Special Needs of International Students in Interlibrary Loans: Some Considerations." *Reference Librarian*, no. 45/46 (1994): 111–17.

Is the Customer Always Right? Towson, MD: ALA Video/Library Video Network., 1994 (videocassette featuring Arlene Farber Sirkin, 23 min.).

Isaacson, David. "Library Inreach." *RQ* 23 (fall 1983): 65–74.

Ivey, Allen E. *Intentional Interviewing and Counseling: Facilitating Client Development in a Multicultural Society.* 3d ed. Pacific Grove, CA: Brooks/Cole, 1994.

———. *Microcounseling: Innovations in Interviewing Training.* Springfield, IL: Thomas, 1971.

Ivey, Allen E., and Jerry Anthier. *Microcounseling: Innovations in Interviewing, Counseling, Psychology, and Psychoeducation.* Springfield, IL: Thomas, 1978.

Ivey, Allen E., Norma B. Gluckstern, and Mary Bradford Ivey. *Basic Attending Skills.* 3d ed. North Amherst, MA: Microtraining Associates, 1992.

Jahoda, Gerald. "Some Unanswered Questions." *Reference Librarian*, no. 1/2 (fall/winter 1981): 159.

Jahoda, Gerald, and Frank Bonney. "The Use of Paraprofessionals in Public Libraries for Answering Reference Queries." *RQ* 29 (spring 1990): 328–31.

Jennerich, Edward J. "The Art of the Reference Interview." *Indiana Libraries* 1 (spring 1981): 7–18.

Jennerich, Edward J., and Elaine Z. Jennerich. "Teaching the Reference Interview." *Journal of Education for Librarianship* 17 (fall 1976): 106–11.

Jennerich, Elaine Zaremba. "Before the Answer: Evaluating the Reference Process." *RQ* 19 (summer 1980): 360–66.

———. "Microcounseling in Library Education." Ph.D. diss., University of Pittsburgh, 1974.

Jennerich, Elaine Zaremba, and Edward J. Jennerich. *The Reference Interview as a Creative Art.* Littleton, CO: Libraries Unlimited, 1987.

Johnson, Nancy. "Questioning Etiquette." *Gifted Child Today* 13 (November–December 1990): 10–11.

Jones, Patrick. "Young and Restless in the Library." *American Libraries* 26 (November 1995): 1038–40.

Katz, Bill, and Ruth A. Fraley, eds. *Conflicts in Reference Services.* New York: Haworth Press, 1985.

Katz, William A. *Introduction to Reference Work.* Vol. 2, *Reference Services and Reference Processes*, 3d ed. New York: McGraw-Hill, 1978 (4th ed., 1982; 5th ed., 1987; 6th ed., 1992).

Kazlauskas, Edward. "An Exploratory Study: A Kinesic Analysis of Academic Library Public Service Points." *Journal of Academic Librarianship* 2, no. 3 (July 1976): 130–34.

Kemp, Jan, and Dennis Dillon. "Collaboration and the Accuracy Imperative: Improving Reference Service Now." *RQ* 29 (fall 1989): 62–70.

Kids Are Patrons Too! Chicago: ALA Video, 1987 (videocassette, 15 min.).

King, Geraldine B. "Open and Closed Questions: The Reference Interview." *RQ* 12 (winter 1972): 157–60.

Kleinke, Chris L. *First Impressions: The Psychology of Encountering Others.* Englewood Cliffs, NJ: Prentice-Hall, 1975.

Knapp, Sara D. "The Reference Interview in the Computer-Based Setting." *RQ* 17 (summer 1978): 320–24.

Lam, Errol R. "The Reference Interview: Some Intercultural Considerations." *RQ* 27 (spring 1988): 390–95.

Lamprecht, Sandra J. "Online Searching and the Patron: Some Communication Challenges." *Reference Librarian* 16 (winter 1986): 177–84.

Lange, Jovian. "The Great Joy." *Reference Librarian*, no. 1/2 (fall/winter 1981): 163.

Lanning, Scott. "What Does a Reference Librarian Do?" *Library Quarterly* 11, no. 4 (1991): 25–28.

Larason, Larry, and Judith Schiek Robinson. "The Reference Desk: Service Point or Barrier?" *RQ* 23 (spring 1984): 332–49.

Larson, Carole A., and Laura K. Dickson. "Developing Behavioral Reference Desk Performance Standards." *RQ* 33 (spring 1994): 349–57.

Lederman, Linda Costigan. "Fear of Talking: Which Students in the Academic Library Ask Librarians for Help?" *RQ* 20 (summer 1981): 382–89.

Levy, Philippa. *Interpersonal Skills*. Library Training Guides series. London: Library Association, 1993.

Librarians on the Internet: Impact on Reference Services. Edited by Robin Kinder. New York: Haworth Press, 1994.

"The Library Zone: Where Every Patron Is a V.I.P." Baltimore, MD: Library Video Network, 1981 (videocassette [$\frac{1}{2}$ inch], 9 min.).

Lipow, Anne Grodzins, ed. *Rethinking Reference in Academic Libraries*. Proceedings and Process of Library Solutions Institute No. 2. University of California at Berkeley, June 4–6, 1993. Berkeley, CA: Library Solutions Press, 1993.

Lowenthal, Ralph. "Preliminary Indications of the Relationship Between Reference Morale and Performance." *RQ* 29 (spring 1990): 380–93.

Lukenbill, W. Bernard. "Teaching Helping Relationship Concepts in the Reference Process." *Journal of Education for Librarianship* 18 (fall 1977): 110–20.

Lushington, Nolan, and James M. Kusack. *The Design and Evaluation of Public Library Buildings*. Hamden, CT: Library Professional Publications, 1991.

Lynch, Mary Jo. "Reference Interviews in Public Libraries." *Library Quarterly* 48 (April 1978): 119–42.

Macdonald, Gina, and Elizabeth Sarkodie-Mensah. "ESL Students and American Libraries." *College and Research Libraries* 49 (September 1988): 425–31.

Maloff, Chalda, and Susan M. Wood. *Business and Social Etiquette with Disabled People*. Springfield, IL: Charles C. Thomas, 1988.

"Managing the Problem Patron." In *Library Safety and Security: A Comprehensive Manual for Library Administrators and Police and Security Officers*. Goshen, KY: Campus Crime Prevention Programs, 1992.

Mardikian, Jackie, and Martin Kesselman. "Beyond the Desk: Enhanced Reference Staffing for the Electronic Library." *RSR: Reference Services Review* 23, no. 1 (1995): 21–28.

Markham, Marilyn J., Keith H. Stirling, and Nathan M. Smith. "Librarian Self-Disclosure and Patron Satisfaction in the Reference Interview." *RQ* 22 (spring 1983): 369–74.

Mason, Ellsworth, and Joan Mason. "The Whole Shebang: Comprehensive Evaluation of Reference Operations." In *Evaluation of Reference Services,* edited by Bill Katz and Ruth A. Fraley. New York: Haworth Press, 1984.

Maxfield, David K. *Counselor-Librarianship: A New Departure.* Occasional Papers no. 38. Urbana: University of Illinois Library School, March 1954.

Maximizing Customer Satisfaction. Towson, MD: ALA Video/Library Video Network, 1993 (audiocassette by Arlene Farber Sirkin, 45 min.).

McCabe, Gerald B., ed. *Operations Handbook for the Small Academic Library.* Westport, CT: Greenwood Press, 1989.

McDaniel, Julie Ann, and Judith K. Ohles. *Training Paraprofessionals for Reference Service.* New York: Neal-Schuman, 1993.

McNally, Peter F. "Teaching and Learning the Reference Interview." In *The Reference Interview: Proceedings of the CACUL Symposium of the Reference Interview of the Annual Conference of the Canadian Library Association,* edited by Elizabeth Silvester and Lillian Rider. Montreal: Canadian Library Association, 1977.

Mendelsohn, Jennifer. "Human Help at OPAC Terminals Is User Friendly: A Preliminary Study." *RQ* 34 (winter 1994): 173–90.

Michell, Gillian, and Roma M. Harris. "Evaluating the Reference Interview: Some Factors Influencing Patrons and Professionals." *RQ* 27 (fall 1987): 95–105.

Mika, Joseph J., and Bruce A. Shuman. "Legal Issues Affecting Libraries and Librarians: Employment Law, Liability and Insurance Contracts and Problem Patrons." *American Libraries* 19 (April 1988): 314–17.

Miller, Jeannie P., Julia M. Rholes, and Karen Wielhorski. "Planning Reference Service Points: A Decision-Making Model." *Reference Librarian,* no. 39 (1993): 53–64.

Monroe, Margaret E. *Library Adult Education: The Biography of an Idea.* New York: Scarecrow Press, 1963.

Mood, Terry Ann. "Foreign Students and the Academic Library." *RQ* 22 (winter 1982): 175–80.

Morgan, Linda. "Patron Preference in Reference Service Points." *RQ* 19 (summer 1980): 373–75.

Morgan, Rebecca L. *Calming Upset Customers: Staying Effective During Unpleasant Situations.* Menlo Park, CA: Crisp Publications, 1989.

Mucci, Judith. "Videotape Self-Evaluation in Public Libraries: Experiments in Evaluating Public Services." *RQ* 16 (fall 1976): 33–37.

Munoz, J. L. "Significance of Nonverbal Communication in the Reference Interview." *RQ* 16 (spring 1977): 220–24.

Murfin, Marjorie E., and Charles A. Bunge. "Paraprofessionals at the Reference Desk." *Journal of Academic Librarianship* 14 (March 1988): 10–14.

Murfin, Marjorie E., and Gary M. Gugelchuk. "Development and Testing of a Reference Transaction Assessment Instrument." *College and Research Libraries* 48 (July 1987): 314–38.

Murfin, Marjorie E., and Lubomyr R. Wynar. *Reference Service: An Annotated Bibliographic Guide, Supplement 1976–1982.* Littleton, CO: Libraries Unlimited, 1984.

Naiman, Sandra M. "The Unexamined Interview Is Not Worth Having." *Reference Librarian* 16 (winter 1986): 31–45.

Naismith, Rachael. "Reference Communication: Commonalities in the Worlds of Medicine and Librarianship." *College and Research Libraries* 57 (January 1996): 44–57.

Nardi, Bonnie A, Vicki O'Day, and Edward J. Valauskas. "Put a Good Librarian, Not Software, in Driver's Seat." *Christian Science Monitor* (June 4, 1996): 18.

Natowitz, Allen. "International Students in U.S. Academic Libraries: Recent Concerns and Trends." *Research Strategies* 13 (1995): 4–16.

Needham, William L. "Academic Library Service to Handicapped Students." *Journal of Academic Librarianship* 3 (November 1977): 273–79.

Neill, S. D. "Problem Solving and the Reference Process." *RQ* 14 (summer 1975): 310–15.

———. "The Reference Process and Certain Types of Memory: Semantic, Episodic, and Schematic." *RQ* 23 (summer 1984): 417–23.

Nolan, Christopher. "Closing the Reference Interview: Implications for Policy and Practice." *RQ* 31 (summer 1992): 513–23.

Oberg, Larry R. "Responses to Hammond: 'Paraprofessionals at the Reference Desk: The End of the Debate.'" *Reference Librarian* 37 (1992): 105–7.

Osborne, Nancy S. "Librarian Humor in Classroom and Reference." ERIC Document #ED349018, 1992 (abstract).

Oser, Fred. "Referens Simplex, or the Mysteries of Reference Interviewing Revealed." *Reference Librarian* 16 (winter 1986): 53–72.

Overmyer, Elizabeth. "Serving the Reference Needs of Children." *Wilson Library Bulletin* 69 (June 1995): 38.

Pack, Nancy C., and Donald D. Foos. "Library Compliance with the Americans with Disabilities Act." *RQ* 32 (winter 1992): 255–67.

Pagell, Ruth A. "The Reference Interview." *Unabashed Librarian* 30, no. 1 (1979): 8.

Patterson, Charles D. "Books Remain Basic." *Reference Librarian*, no. 1/2 (fall/winter 1981): 171–72.

———. "Personality, Knowledge, and the Reference Librarian." In *Reference Services and Technical Services,* edited by Gordon Stevenson and Sally Stevenson. New York: Haworth Press, 1984.

Peck, Theodore P. "Counseling Skills Applied to Reference Services." *RQ* 14 (spring 1975): 233–35.

Peele, David. "Staffing the Reference Desk." *Library Journal* 105 (September 1980): 1708–11.

Penland, Patrick R. *Interviewing for Counselor and Reference Librarians.* Pittsburgh, PA: University of Pittsburgh, 1970.

Pierson, Robert. "Appropriate Settings for Reference Service." *Reference Services Review* 13 (fall 1985): 13–29.

———. "On Reference Desks." *RQ* 17 (winter 1977): 137–38.

"Problem Patron Manual." Seattle, WA: Odegaard Undergraduate Library, University of Washington, 1991 (unpublished).

Promis, Patricia, and Maria Segura Hoopes. *¿Habla Español? No, But I Can Try to Help You: Practical Spanish for the Reference Desk.* Chicago: RASD/American Library Association, 1991.

Quality Service in the Public Sector. West Des Moines, IA: American Media, n.d. (videotape [VHS], 24 min.).

Radcliff, Carolyn J. "Interpersonal Communication with Library Patrons: Physician-Patient Research Models." *RQ* 34 (summer 1995): 497–506.

Radford, Marie. "Interpersonal Communication Theory in the Library Context: A Review of Current Perspectives." In *Library and Information Science Annual* vol. 5. Littleton, CO: Libraries Unlimited, 1989.

Rapoza, Rita S. "Teaching Communication Skills." *RQ* 10 (spring 1971): 218–20.

Reference and Adult Services Division, Ad Hoc Committee on Behavioral Guidelines for Reference and Information Services. "RASD Draft Guidelines: Proposed Behavioral Standards for Reference and Information Service." *RASD Update* (January-March 1994): 15–17.

Reference and Adult Services Division, American Library Association. "Guidelines for Library Service to Older Adults." *RQ* 26 (summer 1987): 444–47.

Reference and Adult Services Division, American Library Association. "Guidelines for Medical, Legal, and Business Responses at General Reference Desks." *RQ* 31 (summer 1992): 554–55.

Reference and Adult Services Division, American Library Association. "Information Services for Information Consumers: Guidelines for Providers." *RQ* 30 (winter 1990): 262–65.

Reference and Adult Services Division, American Library Association. *Research in Reference Effectiveness.* RASD Occasional Papers no. 16; series edited by Marjorie Murfin and Jo Bell Whitlach. Chicago: American Library Association, 1993.

"Reference—More Than an Answer." Milwaukee, WI: Library Council of Metropolitan Milwaukee, 1975 (videocassette [¾ inch], 20 min.).

Rettig, James. "Behavioral Guidelines for Reference Librarians." *RQ* 31 (fall 1992): 5–7.

Ricks, Thomas, Sheri Orth, Johnathan Buckely, and Marsha D. Broadway. "Finding the Real Information Need: An Evaluation of Reference Negotiation Skills." *Public Libraries* 30 (May/June 1992): 159–61.

Riechel, Rosemarie. "The Telephone Patron and the Reference Interview: The Public Library Experience." *Reference Librarian* 16 (winter 1986): 81–88.

Robinson, Barbara M. "Reference Services: A Model of Question Handling." *RQ* 29 (fall 1989): 48–61.

Rohlf, Robert H. "Setting Your House in Order." In *Library Building Projects: Tips for Survival,* edited by Susan B. Hagloch. Englewood, CO: Libraries Unlimited, 1994. First published in *American Libraries* 20 (April 1989): 304–5.

Ross, Catherine Sheldrick. "How to Find Out What People Really Want to Know." *Reference Librarian* 16 (winter 1986): 19–30.

Ross, Catherine Sheldrick, and Patricia Dewdney. "Best Practices: An Analysis of the Best (and Worst) in 52 Public Library Reference Transactions." *Public Libraries* 33 (September/October 1994): 261–66.

———. *Communicating Professionally: A How-to-Do-It Manual for Library Applications.* New York: Neal-Schuman, 1989.

———. "Reference Interview Skills: Twelve Common Questions." *Public Libraries* 25 (spring 1986): 7–9.

Rubin, Rhea Joyce. "Anger in the Library: Defusing Angry Patrons at the Reference Desk (and Elsewhere)." *Reference Librarian,* no. 31 (1990): 39–51.

Salter, Charles A., and Jeffrey L. Salter. *On the Front Lines: Coping with the Library's Problem Patrons.* Englewood, CO: Libraries Unlimited, 1988.

Schobert, Tim. "Term Paper Counseling: Individualized Bibliographic Instruction." *RQ* 22 (winter 1982): 146–51.

Schwartz, Diane G., and Dottie Eakin. "Reference Service Standards, Performance Criteria, and Evaluation." *Journal of Academic Librarianship* 12 (March 1986): 4–8.

Sexton, Katherine. "Reference Interview and the Young Adult." *Top of the News* 30 (June 1974): 415–19.

Sherrer, Johannah. "Implications of New and Emerging Technologies on Reference Services." In *The Impact of Emerging Technologies on Reference Service and Bibliographic Instruction,* edited by Gary M. Pitkin. Westport, CT: Greenwood Press, 1995.

Silvester, Elizabeth, and Lillian Rider, eds. *The Reference Interview: Proceedings of the CACUL Symposium on the Reference Interview of the Annual Conference of the Canadian Library Association, Montreal, June, 1977.* Montreal: Canadian Library Association, 1977.

Sirkin, Arlene Farber. "Implementing a Total Quality Management Program." *Journal of Library Administration* 18, no. 1/2 (1993): 71–83.

Slavens, Thomas P. *Reference Interviews: Questions and Materials.* 3d ed. Metuchen, NJ: Scarecrow Press, 1994.

Smith, Lisa L. "Evaluating the Reference Interview: A Theoretical Discussion of the Desirability and Achievability of Evaluation." *RQ* 31 (fall 1991): 75–81.

Smith, N. M., and I. Adams, "Using Active Listening to Deal with Problem Patrons." *Public Libraries* 30 (July/August 1991): 236–39.

Smith, Nathan M., and G. Hugh Allred. "Recognizing and Coping with the Vertical Patron." *Special Libraries* 67 (November 1976): 528–33.

Smith, Nathan M., and Steven D. Fitt. "Active Listening at the Reference Desk." *RQ* 21 (spring 1982): 247–49.

Sprules, Marcia L. "Conflicts between Reference and Interlibrary Loan." In *Conflicts in Reference Services*, edited by Bill Katz and Ruth A. Fraley. New York: Haworth Press, 1985.

St. Clair, Guy, and Joan Williamson. *Managing the New One-Person Library*. New York: Bowker Saur, 1992.

St. Clair, Jeffrey W., and Rao Aluri. "Staffing the Reference Desk: Professionals or Nonprofessionals?" *Journal of Academic Librarianship* 3 (July 1977): 149–53.

St. Lifer, Evan. "How Safe Are Our Libraries?" *Library Journal* 119 (August 1994): 35–39.

Standards Committee, Reference and Adult Services Division, American Library Association. "A Commitment to Information Services: Developmental Guidelines." *RQ* 18 (spring 1979): 275–78.

"Standards for College Libraries, 1986." *College and Research Libraries News* 47 (March 1986): 189–200.

Steig, Margaret. "In Defense of Problems: The Classical Method of Teaching." *Journal of Education for Librarianship* 20 (winter 1980): 171–83.

Stephenson, Mary Sue. *Planning Library Facilities: A Selected, Annotated Bibliography*. Metuchen, NJ: Scarecrow Press, 1990.

Stevenson, Gordon, and Sally Stevenson, eds. *Reference Services and Technical Services*. New York: Haworth Press, 1984.

Stover, Mark. "Confidentiality and Privacy in Reference Service." *RQ* 27 (winter 1987): 240–44.

Strickland, Charlene. "Young Users." *Wilson Library Bulletin* 63 (May 1989): 96–97.

Stroud, Elvin E. "Readers' Services—One and All." In *The Librarian and Reference Service,* selected by Arthur Ray Rowland. Hamden, CT: Shoe String Press, 1977.

Stueart, Robert D., and John Taylor Eastlick. *Library Management.* 2d ed. Littleton, CO: Libraries Unlimited, 1981.

Stueart, Robert D., and Barbara B. Moran. *Library and Information Center Management.* 4th ed. Englewood, CO: Libraries Unlimited, 1993.

"Suggestions for the Reader's Advisory Interview." Reading Guidance Institute Papers, 29 June–2 July. Madison: University of Wisconsin Library School, 1965.

Taylor, Robert S. "Question-Negotiation and Information Seeking in Libraries." *College and Research Libraries* 29 (May 1968): 178–94.

Telephone Courtesy Pays Off. West Des Moines, IA: American Media, 1991 (videocassette, 19 min.).

Tenopir, Carol, and Ralf Neufang. "The Impact of Electronic Reference on Reference Librarians." *Online* 16 (May 1992): 54–60.

Thomas, Diana M., Ann T. Hinckley, and Elizabeth R. Eisenbach. *The Effective Reference Librarian.* New York: Academic Press, 1981.

Thompson, Mark J., Nathan M. Smith, and Bonnie L. Woods. "A Proposed Model of Self-Disclosure." *RQ* 20 (winter 1980): 160–64.

Timko, Lola. "Teaching Communication with Problem Patrons in Emergency Situations." *Journal of Education for Librarianship* 19 (winter 1978): 244–46.

Todaro, Julie Beth. "Make 'Em Smile." *School Library Journal* 41 (January 1995): 24–27.

Trejo, Tamiye Fujibayashi, and Mary Kaye. "The Library as a Port of Entry." *American Libraries* 19 (November 1988): 890–92.

Turner, Anne M. *It Comes with the Territory: Handling Problem Situations in Libraries.* Jefferson, NC: McFarland, 1993.

Tyckoson, David A. "Wrong Questions, Wrong Answers: Behavioral vs. Factual Evaluation of Reference Service." *Reference Librarian*, no. 38 (1992): 151–73.

Van Fleet, Connie. "A Matter of Focus: Reference Services for Older Adults." *Reference Librarian*, no. 49/50 (1995): 147–64.

Vavrek, Bernard. "Reference Evaluation: What the 'Guidelines' Don't Indicate." *RQ* 18 (summer 1979): 335–40.

Velleman, Ruth A. *Serving Physically Disabled People: An Information Handbook for All Libraries.* New York: R. R. Bowker, 1979.

Von Seggern, Marilyn. "Evaluating the Interview." *RQ* 29 (winter 1989): 260–65.

Walling, Linda Lucas, and Marilyn M. Irwon, eds. *Information Services for People with Developmental Disabilities.* Westport, CT: Greenwood Press, 1992.

Watstein, Sarah Barbara. "Burnout: From a Librarian's Perspective." ERIC Document #ED195232, 1979: 40p.

Wayman, Sally G. "The International Student in the Academic Library." *Journal of Academic Librarianship* 9 (January 1984): 336–41.

Wertheimer, Leonard. "Library Services to Ethnocultural Minorities: Philosophical and Social Bases and Professional Implications." *Public Libraries* 23 (fall 1987): 98–102.

"When You Meet a Disabled Person." Seattle: University of Washington, Disabled Student Services, November 1988 (brochure).

Whitaker, Cathy Seitz. "Pile-up at the Reference Desk: Teaching Users to Use CD-ROMs." *Laserdisk Professional* 3 (March 1990): 30–34.

White, Emilei C. "Student Assistants in Academic Libraries: From Reluctance to Reliance." *Journal of Academic Librarianship* 11 (May 1985): 93–97.

White, Herbert S. *At the Crossroads: Librarians on the Information Superhighway.* Englewood, CO: Libraries Unlimited, 1995.

———. "The Reference Librarian as Information Intermediary: The Correct Approach Is the One That Today's Client Needs Today." *Reference Librarian*, no. 37 (1992): 23–35.

White, Marilyn Domas. "The Dimensions of the Reference Interview." *RQ* 20 (summer 1981): 373–81.

———. "Evaluation of the Reference Interview." *RQ* 25 (fall 1985): 76–84.

Whitlatch, Jo Bell. "Customer Service: Implications for Reference Practice." *Reference Librarian*, no. 49/50 (1995): 5–24.

———. "Reference Service Effectiveness." *RQ* 30 (winter 1990): 205–20.

———. *The Role of the Academic Reference Librarian.* New York: Greenwood Press, 1990.

———. "Unobtrusive Studies and the Quality of Academic Library Reference Services." *College and Reference Libraries* 50 (March 1989): 181–94.

Whitson, William L. "Differentiated Service: A New Reference Model." *Journal of Academic Librarianship* 21 (March 1995): 103–10.

"Who's First? You're Next, or, How Do You Handle a Busy Reference Desk?" Baltimore, MD: Library Video Network, 1980 (videocassette [½ inch], 29 min.).

Wilson, Patrick. "The Face Value Rule in Reference Work." *RQ* 25 (summer 1986): 468–75.

Woodard, Beth S. "Training, Development, and Continuing Education for the Reference Staff." In *Reference and Information Services*, edited by Richard E. Bopp and Linda C. Smith. Englewood, CO: Libraries Unlimited, 1991.

Woodard, Beth S., and Sharon J. Van Der Laan. "Training Preprofessionals for Reference Service." *Reference Librarian* 16 (winter 1986): 233–54.

Wright, Keith C., and Judith F. Davie. *Library and Information Services for Handicapped Individuals.* 3d ed. Englewood, CO: Libraries Unlimited, 1989.

Wu, Connie, comp. "American Library Terminology—A Guide for International Students." ERIC Document #ED308863, 1988.

Yates, Rochelle. *A Librarian's Guide to Telephone Reference Service.* Hamden, CT: Library Professional Publications/Shoe String Press, 1986.

Young, William F. "Methods for Evaluating Reference Desk Performance." *RQ* 25 (fall 1985): 69–75.

Zipkowitz, Fay. "'No One Wants to See Them': Meeting the Reference Needs of the Deinstitutionalized." *Reference Librarian*, no. 31 (1990): 53–67.

Index